ARROW

HEROES AND VILLAINS

Arrow: Heroes and Villains
ISBN: 9781783295234

Published by Titan Books
A division of Titan Publishing Group Ltd.
144 Southwark St.
London
SE1 0UP

First edition: January 2015

10 9 8 7 6 5 4 3 2 1

To receive advance information, news, competitions, and exclusive offers online,
please sign up for the Titan newsletter on our website: www.titanbooks.com

Did you enjoy this book? We love to hear from our readers. Please e-mail us
at: readerfeedback@titanemail.com or write to Reader Feedback at the above
address.

A CIP catalogue record for this title is available from the British Library.

Printed and bound in the USA.

ARROW

HEROES AND VILLAINS

TITAN BOOKS

CONTENTS

INTRODUCTION

As the popular Super Hero television show *Smallville* neared the end of its impressive ten-season run in 2011, Warner Bros. Television and the CW Network announced that they would be making a brand new series: *Arrow*. Developed by the talented trio of Greg Berlanti, Marc Guggenheim, and Andrew Kreisberg, *Arrow* is based on the longtime DC Comics Super Hero Green Arrow (real name: Oliver Queen). While Green Arrow had been a regular character in the final seasons of *Smallville*, the new series started fresh when it debuted in the fall of 2012, creating a brand-new mythology with no ties to the world of *Smallville*.

According to Guggenheim, that was the intention for *Arrow* all along. "We loved *Smallville*, and we loved the version of Oliver Queen that was in *Smallville*," he says, "but the truth of the matter is that we wanted to do our own thing and not be beholden to prior continuity, looks, and tones." Since this television show did not come about as a spinoff of *Smallville*, one might wonder how Green Arrow was selected from DC Comics' stable of characters to star in his own show. The reason is twofold. "It was because the character doesn't have any superpowers and is basically a normal guy with a lot of training," Guggenheim reveals. "And the other element of the character is the fact that Green Arrow's origin takes place over the course of years. He developed his archery

skills while marooned on a deserted island. One of the key elements of Greg Berlanti's original take was that we would basically meet Oliver Queen as he becomes Green Arrow, but then we would flashback over the course of the series to his time on that island, honing his skills and becoming the man that we're seeing on screen in the present day. There are not a lot of Super Heroes, if any, really, who have the kind of origin story that can be played out over the course of several years. And that's something television does really well, because it's an open-ended medium."

While the essence of the source material remains the same, *Arrow* does differ from the comics in several ways. For one, the name Green Arrow is never mentioned on the show, other than a winking in-joke in an early season 1 conversation between Oliver Queen and Malcolm Merlyn. In early episodes, the citizens of Starling City refer to the masked vigilante roaming their streets first as simply the Vigilante, then as the Hood, and then in season 2 he becomes the Arrow.

Most notably, the executive producers wanted the show's version of the character to be as down to earth as possible. "Our goal wasn't so much about downplaying superpowers, as it was that we just wanted to do something really grounded and make it real," Guggenheim says. For instance, in the comic books, the

"**THOSE** WHO **RULE** MY **CITY** THROUGH **INTIMIDATION** AND **FEAR**, EVERY **ONE** OF THEM WILL WISH I HAD **DIED** ON THAT **ISLAND**."

The Arrow wearing his signature costume, complete with greasepaint.

name of the government organization A.R.G.U.S. stands for Advanced Research Group Uniting Superhumans, but on the show it stands for Advanced Research Group United Support. "We introduced A.R.G.U.S. in season 1 of *Arrow* and we didn't have a world with superpowers, so it seemed impossible to have this organization be all about superhumans on a show that at the time didn't really have any plans to ever show superhumans."

Similarly, the name of Oliver Queen's hometown was changed from Star City to Starling City. "That was also just to further ground the show," Guggenheim confirms. "Star City was a name that was developed back in what was known as the Silver Age of comic books, in the 1950s, where things were very fantastical and there was a big sci-fi influence on comics at the time. Star City just didn't sound like a realistic city, it sounded like a science-fiction city, and we were trying to ground *Arrow* in every way."

And then—in a *flash*—superpowers snuck into the show, or at least the hint of them, when Barry Allen appeared in season 2. "The decision was made to spinoff *The Flash* and to introduce Barry Allen in two episodes of *Arrow*," notes Guggenheim. "So we moved in that direction. In order to introduce Barry and the concept of superpowers, we had to alter the show a bit, and that's when we introduced the mirakuru serum that plays so prominently in season 2. For my money, the mirakuru serum is the 'Arrowified' version of superpowers. We grounded it in as much fake science as we could and we didn't give it a comic book-sounding name; we gave it a

Japanese name. No one's flying around, no one's shooting laser beams out of their eyes. As superpowers go, the mirakuru soldiers of season 2 were pretty grounded. And now that we've done that, now that there's an entire show with The Flash, where superpowers can exist, in season 3 we're returning *Arrow* to its origins of being very superpower-free, as it were."

Another way they grounded the character was with his costume. "We didn't want it to look like a costume, per se," Guggenheim says, "we wanted Oliver to walk down the street in costume and not get stares. If you look at his costume you'll see that it's mostly a leather jacket with a hood on it. Oliver really could pop the hood up and unzip the jacket and be wearing a regular outfit for the most part." As long as he remembered to take his mask off, of course, which in the first season would've required a good handkerchief.

"The greasepaint 'mask' from the first season-and-a-half was actually Greg's idea," Guggenheim reveals. "We'd had a lot of discussions about, 'How do we conceal his identity if we don't have a mask? Is the hood going to be enough to obscure his face?' And in prep, Greg came up with this idea of using the greasepaint, which I really thought was brilliant. We always say, 'What's the *Arrow* version of what we're trying to do?' And for my money, the eye make-up was the *Arrow* version of a comic-book mask. It was so clever and in keeping with the grounded nature of the show." Nonetheless, in season 2, Oliver donned a mask specially designed for him by Barry Allen.

Oliver Queen transformed himself from a scared young man into a deadly vigilante.

"There's no way to make a mask look like you're not playing to the Super Hero convention of masks, but we felt we'd earned the right to give him a mask in season 2," Guggenheim explains. "And thus we did."

Arrow's version of Oliver Queen differs in another fundamental way from previous incarnations, at least initially: this vigilante has no qualms with killing bad guys, as long as they deserve it. This also sets him apart from nearly every other Super Hero ever depicted on television, and the toll this decision takes on Oliver's soul was one of the key themes running throughout the first season of the show.

As *Arrow* begins, Oliver Queen returns home to Starling City after a shipwreck in the South Pacific five years earlier, which left him and everyone else aboard—including his father—missing and presumed dead. While it's clear to Oliver's family and friends that his time on the presumedly deserted island changed him, no one knows just how much. The former billionaire party boy now spends his nights as a masked vigilante, working to bring the city's many high-powered, super-rich robber barons to justice. The first season of *Arrow* is devoted primarily to these two overarching storylines: Oliver's quest for vigilante justice, and his family and friends' quest to reconnect with the man they once knew. Along the way, flashbacks to Oliver's time on the island are sprinkled liberally throughout nearly every episode, giving the audience an opportunity to see just how and why Oliver underwent such a thorough transformation from a spoiled, entitled jerk into a coldblooded killer.

The first season ends in spectacular fashion as a shadowy cabal of Starling City's elite, spearheaded by Malcolm Merlyn (father of Oliver's best friend Tommy) and Oliver's own mother, Moira Queen, work to destroy the Glades, a poor, crime-ridden neighborhood, with a momentous seismic event known as the Undertaking. Oliver is able to stop the scheme, but not before half the neighborhood is destroyed in an earthquake. By the time the dust settles, Malcolm and Tommy Merlyn are

dead, and Moira is in jail after publicly revealing her involvement in the dastardly plot.

"I have a great amount of affection for season 1's finale episode," Guggenheim reflects. "That was an episode where everything came together—it had heart and it had emotion and it had scope. I remember the episode airing and thinking, 'We'll never be able to top this.' And while I think that we have since gone on and topped it, that feeling that this was the pinnacle of the show was very convincing to me and it'll always have a special place in my heart."

Following Tommy's death, Oliver vows to use nonlethal methods to fight crime; his struggle with that vow is a strong undercurrent throughout the show's fantastic second season. The flashbacks on the island increasingly connect directly with the present-day storylines in season two, as Oliver's friends from the island, who were thought long dead, reappear in Starling City, now very much alive. Oliver also deals with the fallout from his mother's role in the Undertaking, as well as an attempt by outside groups to oust him and his family from their role as the heads of Queen Consolidated.

Oliver's crime-fighting family also grows in season 2, as he takes in his sister's boyfriend (and aspiring vigilante) Roy Harper as a protégé, and Sara Lance joins as the Canary, both heroes being key components in the Green Arrow comic mythos.

Like those in any great television series, the characters of *Arrow* drive the story much more than the heroic deeds and villainous machinations on screen every week. Oliver's family and ever-expanding circle of friends and confidants are well-drawn, deep, rich characters whose actions always come from somewhere that's true to who they are. When they do things and say things, it's not because the plot needs them to, but because that's *who they are*.

These are the heroes and villains of *Arrow*.

OLIVER QUEEN

Oliver Jonas Queen is the eldest child of Robert and Moira Queen. In their early twenties, Oliver and his best friend Tommy Merlyn were stereotypical spoiled rich kids. The two young men found themselves embroiled in one scandal after another: assaulting paparazzi, stealing taxis, and urinating on police officers. Some of their other friends who would turn up later on *Arrow* included McKenna Hall and the Lance sisters, Laurel and Sara.

Five years prior to the start of the series, Oliver was dating Laurel Lance. When she brought up the idea of moving in together, Oliver panicked, and made a series of bad decisions. One of these was sleeping with another woman and getting her pregnant; his mother got him out of that jam by paying the woman $2 million to never be heard from again. Oliver also began sleeping with Laurel's sister Sara, even going so far as inviting her to sneak away with him aboard his family yacht, the *Queen's Gambit*, as his father sailed to China on a business trip.

But the boat never made it to China, instead sinking somewhere in the Pacific Ocean. When it was all over, Oliver had washed up ashore the island of Lian Yu, believing himself to be the only survivor. He couldn't help but suffer from survivor's guilt—feeling responsible for bringing Sara along, and having watched his father shoot himself in the head while they floated in a lifeboat, just

so the meager food and water supplies they'd salvaged would last longer. But before he made this sacrificial gesture, Robert Queen demanded that Oliver survive so that he could right Robert's wrongs.

Executive Producer Greg Berlanti has this to say about Oliver's relationship with his family: "Oliver has always had a blind spot where his family is concerned. In his days as a carefree billionaire playboy, pre-island, he lived in a constant haze of parties and girls. He really didn't think about what was going on with them. This changed when his father killed himself on the raft to save him. Robert Queen told him to be a better man than he was and to right his wrongs. This woke Oliver up and started his year-one journey. The sins of the father soon led to the sins of the mother, as Oliver discovered that she wasn't who he thought she was either. Oliver truly loved his parents, but had to reconcile how to forgive them."

While burying his father on the island, Oliver found a notebook in Robert's pocket that contained a list of names Oliver would later learn were a group of robber barons and corporate raiders who were poisoning Starling City with their unethical business practices. Stopping the people on this list before they could further harm Starling City became the foundation of the Arrow persona Oliver would adopt upon his return to civilization five years later.

FACT SHEET

Portrayed by: Stephen Amell

Aliases: The Starling City Vigilante, the Hood, the Arrow

Current Status: alive, CEO of Queen Consolidated

Relationships: Robert and Moira Queen (parents, both deceased), Thea Queen (half-sister), John Diggle, Felicity Smoak, Roy Harper, Sara Lance, Quentin Lance (partners in crime-fighting), Laurel Lance (ex-girlfriend)

History: Green Arrow first appeared in the comics way back in 1941, in *More Fun Comics* #73, and has been a mainstay in DC Comics' stable of Super Heroes ever since.

"TO LIVE, I HAD TO MAKE MYSELF MORE THAN WHAT I WAS, TO FORGE MYSELF INTO A WEAPON."

But before all that, Oliver had to survive on the island, which would not be easy, as shortly after he arrived he was shot in the shoulder with an arrow by a man in a green hood named Yao Fei. But Yao Fei chose not to kill him, instead taking Oliver under his wing and teaching him survival skills, including hunting with a bow and arrow. This would certainly become significant later on.

A few days later Oliver was captured by a group of armed mercenaries led by Edward Fyers, who first questioned, then tortured him in order to get information on Yao Fei's whereabouts. Oliver didn't crack, surviving long enough for Yao Fei to rescue him and return Oliver to his camp before leaving him alone again.

Not long after, Oliver met another lone figure in the island jungle—Slade Wilson. The men soon bonded over their common friend, Yao Fei, and their shared goal of commandeering a supply plane and escaping the island. Slade picked up Oliver's training where Yao Fei had left off, instructing Oliver in the arts of combat and strategy. They were later joined by Yao Fei's daughter, Shado, who instructed Oliver in archery, insisting that he had to learn to shoot if they had any hope of ever getting off the island.

Not long after Oliver's archery lesson, the trio were shocked to see Yao Fei march into their camp followed closely by Fyers' men, who took them all captive and brought them to their compound. Fyers revealed that his

mission on the island was to shoot down a Ferris Air jet bound for China in an effort to destabilize the Chinese economy. He threatened to kill Shado if Yao Fei did not record a video claiming responsibility for the terrorist attack, which was the final piece of this mission's puzzle. Yao Fei agreed to record the statement in order to save his daughter's life. As soon as he was finished, however, Fyers put a bullet in his head.

Using a knife Yao Fei had slipped him just before his death, Oliver cut himself and his friends free, and they were able to redirect the missile Fyers had planned for the Ferris jet, destroying Fyers' camp instead. Oliver then found Yao Fei's bow and put an arrow in Fyers' heart, killing him. This marks the moment when Oliver shows he has the strength to survive on Lian Yu. Greg Berlanti says, "Oliver's transition on the island was based on the necessity to survive and return home. He had to evolve to survive both for him and his father's sacrifice."

The trio lived peacefully on Lian Yu for a while afterwards, and Oliver grew close romantically to Shado, which Slade interpreted as weakness. That peace was shattered by the arrival of another group of mercenaries—this one brought to the island by Dr. Anthony Ivo aboard the freighter *Amazo*. Ivo had come to Lian Yu in search of mirakuru, a WWII-era serum designed to give Japanese soldiers superhuman abilities.

Oliver may not have any superpowers, but he does have access to an incredible array of technology and weaponry thanks to his vast wealth.

But the *Amazo* brought someone else to Lian Yu as well: Sara Lance. Oliver was shocked to see her aboard the freighter, as he had assumed she was dead and lost at sea when the *Queen's Gambit* sank. After Sara helped Oliver escape captivity on the freighter, she joined the group on the island as they agreed to find the mirakuru in order to save Slade, who was slowly dying from his collective injuries from battles with Ivo's men.

Oliver's crew found the serum aboard the wreckage of a Japanese submarine and injected Slade with it, but not before the older man revealed that he had been in love with Shado the entire time she and Oliver had been together. Then, blood poured from his eyes, his pulse slowed, then stopped. Ivo's men arrived immediately after and took Oliver, Shado, and Sara captive once more. Ivo presented Oliver with a horrible choice: to choose which of the two women to save, as Ivo would kill the other. If he chose neither, Ivo would kill them both.

When Oliver couldn't choose, Ivo raised his gun to make good on his threat to kill both women. It looked like Ivo was going to shoot Sara first, so Oliver dove between her and the gun. Interpreting this as Oliver's choice, Ivo immediately executed Shado. Slade suddenly reappeared, reanimated and mirakuru-enhanced. Seeing Shado's body,

he slipped into a black rage and killed all of Ivo's men, but the doctor managed to escape into the jungle.

Oliver and Slade buried Shado on the beach next to Yao Fei and Robert Queen, and Slade gave Shado's green hood to Oliver. Slade, Sara, and Oliver then headed to the freighter to take care of Ivo once and for all. But once aboard the ship, Slade learned the full truth of how Shado died. Something in his brain snapped, and he turned on Oliver. Along with some prisoners he and Sara rescued, Oliver escaped overboard, but Slade took control of the ship. Blaming the mirakuru for his friend's actions, Oliver returned to the ship to find Ivo's cure for the serum, with the intention of saving Slade. Sara insisted on joining him, only to be lost at sea once more as a torpedo from the submarine caused the *Amazo* to sink. Horrified by Sara's apparent death, Oliver chose to kill Slade instead of giving him the cure. After a falling pile of rubble crushed Slade, Oliver drove an arrow through his eye, leaving him aboard the sinking ship, headed for the bottom of the sea.

Four years later, Oliver was rescued from Lian Yu by a small Chinese fishing boat, and he returned to Starling City. Almost immediately upon his return home, Oliver began a vigilante crusade against the names on his father's list.

"WELL, YOU KNOW us **BILLIONAIRE VIGILANTES...** WE DO **LOVE OUR TOYS."**

Despite some initial frustrations, Oliver and Diggle soon formed a close bond forged by mutual respect.

Oliver's first ally in his crusade was John Diggle, his personal security guard. Diggle was wounded by the assassin Deadshot in "Lone Gunmen" (season 1, episode 3), and Oliver brought him to his hideout in an old Queen Consolidated factory (known as the "Arrowcave" or "Foundry") to recuperate, revealing his secret to Diggle in the process. They were later joined by Queen Consolidated computer genius Felicity Smoak, who uses her computer prowess to gather information for the Hood and serve as a technology expert.

Oliver's personal life was much harder to reacclimatize to upon his return, as he had difficulty reconnecting with his mother Moira, his sister Thea, and his best friend Tommy Merlyn. But the biggest difficulty was with Laurel Lance, who harbored an enormous amount of anger for Oliver, holding him responsible for her sister's death. These difficulties were only compounded when Oliver discovered that Laurel and Tommy had begun dating.

Oliver maintained his billionaire playboy persona brilliantly, opening up a nightclub, Verdant, in the ground floors of the Queen Consolidated building above his Arrowcave hideaway, giving him an easy excuse to be in the area at all hours of the day and night.

The pursuit of the names on his father's list led to Oliver uncovering a vast criminal conspiracy that connected his parents and Malcolm Merlyn with some of the biggest names in the Starling City criminal underworld. Malcolm was the mastermind behind the plan, which would see him destroy the crime-ridden Glades neighborhood and rebuild it in a new vision for the city. Malcolm had a secret identity of his own— the Dark Archer—and he battled the Hood on several occasions as Oliver tried to stop the Undertaking.

The Hood's team managed to stop Malcolm's earthquake device, but a second device went off, leaving the entire east side of the neighborhood in ruins. In the aftermath, Tommy saved Laurel, but Oliver was unable to save Tommy; his best friend died in his arms. Meanwhile, Moira was charged with conspiracy to commit mass murder.

Despondent over his failure to prevent the destruction of the Glades, Oliver left Starling City for a few months and journeyed to Lian Yu, only returning home when Queen Consolidated faced a hostile takeover attempt from Isabel Rochev.

Inspired by Tommy's memory, Oliver vowed to no longer kill his enemies, and instead of the Hood, he began calling himself the Arrow.

VIGILANTE OR HERO?

Are the terms vigilante and hero synonymous? Not necessarily. *Arrow* writer and producer Wendy Mericle weighs in on the subject that Super Hero fans have debated since the first masked hero broke the law to deal out their own form of justice. "In the comic books, Green Arrow had that very Robin Hood take-from-the-rich-and-give-to-the-poor mentality," she points out. "And, especially in the first season, we [similarly] came in with a very strong social-justice angle. It's morphed over the course of the two seasons in that it's something that still comes up now and then, but we found it actually difficult to write to that. I think that's one of the things that might live more easily in a comic-book context than it does on television. He's still very much fighting for the underdog, but it just has fewer class overtones on the show; it's more about fighting for people who have no voice. That's something we have been very aware of in building him from vigilante to hero over the course of the first two seasons, and in the third season we're especially going to be working on that element."

In the minds of the show's writers, there is indeed a distinction between vigilante and hero. "One of the things we talked about in season 2 was: 'Does a hero kill people or does he deliver them to the authorities to be served up justice?' I think in this show that is the biggest difference between a hero and a vigilante," says Mericle. "We talk a lot in the writers' room about it. There's no question about the fact that Arrow works outside the law. He might work more closely with the police now, and has [Quentin] Lance working with him, trying to deliver justice, but the whole point of the Arrow, even as a hero, is to do what the cops can't do. And so there's always that tension. That's where the show lives and I think that's a good thing. I think these are interesting moral questions to think about. From a storyteller's point of view, it's so much better not to kill because then those villains can get out and you can have another episode [with them]. Arrow goes against his own season 2 rule and kills Vertigo, but that's because he went after Felicity. And I don't think you can count that as a huge loss for Starling."

There's also an argument that the Arrow is in a war against those who have failed the city. Mericle says: "Dig weighs in on that because of his military background. There's no question—in a war, you *do* kill. You dehumanize the enemy and that's your job." But even in a war, killing people has consequences. "Oliver was a killer in the first season, and we talk about what the ramifications of that are: what does that do to you? What does that do to your soul?"

By the end of his time on Lian Yu, Oliver had become hardened, willing to kill in order to survive.

"I WAS WRONG TO THINK I COULD HAVE IT BOTH WAYS. TO DO WHAT I DO AND HAVE A NORMAL LIFE."

Team Arrow, as Felicity called them, soon grew by two more members. A mysterious female vigilante known as the Canary arrived in Starling City not long after the Undertaking, and the Arrow teamed up with her a few times before uncovering her true identity: Sara Lance, who had once more returned from the dead. Roy Harper, a streetwise kid who began dating Thea Queen, was also added to the team because Oliver was impressed by his heart and desire to help the people of the Glades. Detective Quentin Lance, once the Vigilante's police nemesis, came over to his side, often offering a reciprocal exchange of assistance where needed.

Oliver soon faced his biggest challenge ever as Slade Wilson crawled back into his life, seeking revenge for Shado's death. He kidnapped the entire Queen family and forced Oliver to choose between Moira's and Thea's life. Before he could do so Moira begged Slade to kill her, which he then did.

Oliver had his final showdown with Slade when the latter unleashed his mirakuru army on Starling City. After being cured of the mirakuru by Felicity, a weakened Slade was eventually defeated. Oliver faced the choice of whether or not to kill his old friend. Oliver chose to spare Slade's life and deliver him to an A.R.G.U.S. prison on Lian Yu instead.

STEPHEN AMELL *IS* OLIVER QUEEN

You might think that constantly switching between the young Ollie of the past, the mature present-day Oliver, and the intimidating Arrow would make it challenging for actor Stephen Amell to keep the personalities and voices straight, but that is not the case. "One of the happy surprises of the show," says executive producer Marc Guggenheim, "is just how incredibly apt Stephen is at juggling all these different performances—and he proved this back when we were shooting the pilot. It's really to Stephen's credit that it all hangs together as well as it does without becoming confusing or sloppy. For 'Flashback Oliver' he brings a different tone and even raises the register of his voice slightly, and his physical manner is different; all these things go into distinguishing Oliver in the present day from Oliver in the past."

It was as if the role was tailor-made for Amell. "He was actually the very first person to come in and audition for the pilot," Guggenheim shares. "And not just for Oliver—he was literally the very first audition that we saw. It was undeniable—it was pretty obvious to everybody that he would be Oliver."

ROBERT QUEEN

Robert Queen was the founder and CEO of Queen Consolidated, a multibillion-dollar international corporation. Five years before *Arrow* began, Robert and everyone aboard the *Queen's Gambit,* including his son Oliver, went missing and were presumed dead when the luxury yacht was shipwrecked somewhere in the South Pacific. Robert Queen left behind a wife, Moira, and teenage daughter, Thea.

Although his children didn't realize it, Robert Queen was an unfaithful husband, frequently cheating on his wife throughout their marriage. Moira tried to get back at him by sleeping with his best friend, Malcolm Merlyn, which led to the birth of Thea. In his favor, despite always being aware that Thea was not his daughter, Robert loved her as if she were his own child.

Some years later, Robert fell in love with a young intern at Queen Consolidated, Isabel Rochev. The two had a rather torrid affair, and Robert was even prepared to leave his family for her. But Thea had an accident the night he planned to run away with Isabel, falling off a horse and breaking her arm. Robert went to the hospital, and Isabel gave him an ultimatum: to choose her or his family. Robert made his choice by firing Isabel.

When Queen Consolidated opened a factory in the Glades, a shady city council member approached Robert looking for a payoff to ensure the project ran smoothly. Robert had no interest in bribery, which led to a violent argument that ended with Robert accidentally causing the council member to fall to his death.

Depressed following the incident, Robert turned to his friend Malcolm Merlyn with an idea: to found Tempest, a secret organization that would better Starling City by battling its endemic corruption. Merlyn was dissatisfied with the slow results of this plan, which led him to dream up the Undertaking: a massive earthquake that would destroy the crime-plagued neighborhood of the Glades. Robert was adamantly opposed to the idea, and agreed to meet with Frank Chen, another Tempest member, in China to discuss buying up most of the Glades in order to stop Merlyn. However, Chen betrayed Robert to Merlyn, who then sabotaged the *Queen's Gambit,* causing it to sink en route to China.

Despite dying before the main events of the series even began, Robert Queen's ghost, both literal and figurative, has haunted *Arrow* since the very first episodes. In his final moments aboard a life raft following the shipwreck, Robert begged his son to right his wrongs, asking Oliver to correct the sins of his father.

"I'M **NOT THE MAN** YOU THINK I AM. I DIDN'T BUILD OUR CITY; I **FAILED** IT."

MOIRA QUEEN

Moira Queen is the mother of Oliver and Thea Queen, the widow of Robert Queen, and the ex-wife of former Queen Consolidated CEO Walter Steele. She is also the former lover of Malcolm Merlyn.

Moira was overjoyed when Oliver, thought to be dead for five years following the wreck of the *Queen's Gambit*, returned to Starling City very much alive. In order to keep him safe as he readjusted to civilized life, she hired John Diggle to act as Oliver's bodyguard following a kidnapping attempt. In the first of many duplicitous moments, Moira turned out to be the one behind the abduction, hoping to discern just how much Oliver had learned about Robert's involvement with the Undertaking.

Moira and her shadowy co-conspirators were made very nervous by the arrival of the Starling City Vigilante, who seemed to be targeting not just the rich and powerful, but specifically the individuals named in "The List." Malcolm Merlyn began to suspect Oliver, since both men showed up in Starling City at the same time, but Moira assured him that this was not the case, even after Oliver was arrested by the police and charged with being the Vigilante.

Moira's husband Walter then informed her that he had found the remains of the *Queen's Gambit* in a nondescript Starling City warehouse. Moira told him to drop the matter, which caused Walter to walk out on her, saying he didn't know when he'd be back. Once he did return, he confronted Moira about her copy of the notebook that held "The List," which led to Malcolm having

"I CAN'T FIGHT THEM; I AM THEM."

Moira was a conflicted woman. Though she loved her family deeply, she was not afraid to use underhand methods to get what she wanted.

Walter abducted to keep him from poking his nose any further into the Undertaking.

Malcolm promised Moira that Walter would be unharmed and released after the Undertaking, but unbeknownst to Moira, Diggle overheard this conversation and recorded it for Oliver. The Hood then paid a visit to Moira to confront her about it, only to have his own mother shoot and nearly kill him.

Sensing the sheer insanity of the project, Moira tried to disassociate herself with the Undertaking in "Dodger" (season 1, episode 15), going so far as to hire China White and the Triad gang to kill Malcolm for her. The attempt failed, and Malcolm came to Moira asking her to identify who inside their organization had arranged the hit.

Moira was slow in providing answers, so Malcolm contacted the Triad to set a meeting in "Salvation" (season 1, episode 18) and find out who had paid for the assassination attempt. At this point, Moira gave him the name Frank Chen, the man who had set up her meeting with the Triad in the first place, in order to throw suspicion off herself. Malcolm, in his guise as the Dark Archer, killed Chen, although Moira successfully persuaded him to leave Chen's daughter alive.

In a flashback scene during "The Undertaking" (season 1, episode 19), Robert Queen filled Moira in on Tempest's plan to level the Glades. Moira was rightly horrified, and

begged her then-husband not to do it. Meanwhile, in the present day, Walter was rescued by the Hood. After a happy homecoming, Walter realized that his wife knew more than she was letting on about his abduction, so he surprised her by requesting a divorce.

After Diggle, disguised as the Hood, forced a confession about her involvement in the Undertaking from Moira by torturing her son, Oliver convinced his mother that she had to do something to end the madness. In "Sacrifice" (season 1, episode 23), Moira held a press conference where she admitted her role in the scheme, and was consequently arrested for conspiracy to commit mass murder.

Arrow's second season opened with Moira imprisoned in Iron Heights, awaiting trial for the murder of the 503 residents of the Glades who died during the Undertaking. Although the District Attorney was pushing for the death penalty, Moira refused to take the stand and testify on her own behalf, believing there are some stones best left unturned.

Moira's trial began in "State v. Queen" (season 2, episode 7). She still refused to take the stand, and finally told her children why: if she did, the DA would question her about the affair she had years before with Malcolm Merlyn. Thea and Oliver convinced her that it didn't matter, and that she needed to testify to strengthen her

FACT SHEET

Portrayed by: Susanna Thompson

Aliases: none

Current Status: deceased

Relationships: Robert Queen (husband, deceased), Oliver Queen (son), Thea Queen (daughter), Walter Steele (ex-husband), Malcolm Merlyn (ex-lover)

Comics History: Moira Queen made her DC Comics debut in 1995, appearing in flashbacks in *Green Arrow Annual* #7. She and her husband Robert were mauled by lions in a tragic safari accident, leaving Oliver orphaned and traumatized.

After Walter was kidnapped by Malcolm, Moira became the acting CEO of Queen Consolidated for a time.

defense. In the end, despite the prosecution's strong case, the jury acquitted Moira on all charges.

After her release, she was taken to meet with Malcolm Merlyn, now very much alive after being presumed dead during the Undertaking. Malcolm revealed to Moira that he had manipulated the jury into her acquittal, and, more importantly, that he now knew that Thea was actually his own daughter.

Moira was convinced to run for mayor by Walter and his colleagues in "Tremors" (season 2, episode 12); they believed that front-running candidate Sebastian Blood's policies would be bad for their corporations. Moira was skeptical at first, but Walter shared polls that showed 43 percent of the city did not hold her responsible for the Undertaking, and he also pointed out that everyone loves a good redemption story.

In "Heir to the Demon" (season 2, episode 13) Felicity Smoak figured out Thea's true parentage and confronted Moira about it. Felicity later told Oliver, who went to Moira furious that she had hidden a truth like that for so long. Moira invoked her usual defense—"I did it to protect this family"—but Oliver was not having it, and declared their relationship over.

Things really came to a head for Moira in "Seeing Red" (season 2, episode 20). Thea was no longer speaking with her mother, thanks to Slade Wilson revealing her father's true identity. Rightly sensing that her family was falling apart, Moira scheduled a press conference to announce she was dropping out of the mayoral race. But Oliver convinced her to stay in it, telling Moira that she could then convince Thea she was a decent person by changing Starling City for the good. Moira agreed, and then revealed that she had always known Oliver was the Arrow, but had just never said anything. She also revealed just how proud she was of him and the work he had done.

The Queen family was reunited in a limousine after the press conference, only to be kidnapped by Slade Wilson. Moira was tied up along with Thea and Oliver, and Slade tried to force Oliver to decide which of the women he should kill, a deliberate invocation of the sick game Dr. Ivo had played with Oliver, Sara, and Shado on Lian Yu. Oliver refused to decide, so Moira volunteered herself. Slade remarked on her true courage, saying it was a shame it wasn't passed on to her son, before running her through with a sword in front of her own children.

A MOTHER'S LOVE

With the number of lies she told and the secrets she kept, you might find it hard to know what to believe about Moira Queen, but one thing's for certain: she loved her children more than life, something she proved upon her death. Moira's death shocked many viewers, and left writer-producer Wendy Mericle mourning the passing of a great character. "I understood the importance of doing it from a story point of view, but she had a certain gravitas and I felt that she really made the show interesting," remarks Mericle. "One of my favorite scenes in the pilot, and the one that really hooked me into the show, was when you find out at the end that she was the one who had Oliver kidnapped. Here's this woman who loves her family so much, she's willing to have them tortured in order to make sure that they're safe from the enemies that she herself has made. I really liked the moral complexity of her and her machinations, and her scenes with Malcolm. I really liked all those elements on the show, so I was heartbroken when I saw the staging of the scene and the brutality of it and the unfairness of it. But it made for a very powerful ending for season 2.

"We ended season 1 with Tommy dying, so taking someone off the board like Moira was going to have a tremendous impact. Oliver's family is decimated, and we wanted that at the end [of season 2]. We wanted him to beat Slade, but have a pyrrhic victory and suffer some tremendous losses, so going into season 3 he's carrying the weight of that and it becomes really important for him to get Thea back from wherever she went at the end of season 2. Thea is the last family he has and he has to make sure that he can protect her."

FACT SHEET

Portrayed by: Willa Holland
Aliases: Speedy (affectionate nickname given to her by her brother Oliver)
Current Status: alive
Relationships: Malcolm Merlyn (father), Moira Queen (mother, deceased), Oliver Queen (half-brother), Robert Queen (emotional, if not biological, father), Tommy Merlyn (half-brother, deceased), Roy Harper (ex-boyfriend)

Comics History: Thea Dearden Queen has yet to appear in the comics, as she is an original character created for *Arrow*. However, Mia Dearden is one of Green Arrow's numerous sidekicks, also taking on the name Speedy at one time.

THEA QUEEN

The Queen is Oliver Queen's younger sister, and the daughter of Moira Queen. For most of her life, Thea believed herself to be the daughter of Robert Queen, the man who raised her before his tragic death aboard the *Queen's Gambit*. But that was not the case; Thea's birth father was actually Malcolm Merlyn, her father's best friend and business partner, with whom her mother had had an affair. This revelation rocked Thea to her core, and she now believes she cannot trust anything anyone in her family says anymore.

It wasn't always this way; Thea idolized her older brother Oliver as a child. He gave her the nickname "Speedy" from all the times he chased her around Queen Mansion. Her father and brother's presumed deaths left an adolescent Thea feeling alone and disconnected from the world, and she tried to fill the void by drifting into a world of parties, booze, and drugs.

When Oliver returned after his time on the island of Lian Yu, Thea welcomed him home with open arms. She soon grew angry with her big brother, however, when he disapproved of her hedonistic lifestyle—ironically, the very sort of life he'd been leading when he disappeared five years earlier.

In "Trust but Verify" (season 1, episode 11), Thea became suspicious that Moira was cheating on her stepfather Walter Steele with Malcolm Merlyn.

Despondent at the thought of losing yet another father figure in her life, Thea tried a new drug called Vertigo on her 18th birthday, subsequently crashing her new car and ending up in the hospital. She was then summarily arrested for driving under the influence.

The judge at Thea's trial in "Vertigo" (season 1, episode 12) made the decision that the best way to discourage the use of Vertigo was to show that not even the wealthy are above the law, and sentenced Thea to jail time. Detective Quentin Lance was able to get Thea out of jail in exchange for 500 hours of community service under the watchful eye of his daughter, Laurel, at Laurel's legal aid center.

Thea was mugged for her purse in "Dodger" (season 1, episode 15). Using the legal resources now at her disposal, she tracked down the thief, Roy Harper, and visited him at his home in the Glades. Roy blew her off, and when she returned to give him a piece of her mind, he brushed her off again, only to follow after her and save her from being attacked by some street thugs. In doing so, Roy was stabbed, and Thea rushed him to the hospital. In order to distract him from his fear of being injected, Thea kissed Roy, and their romance bloomed from there.

Following Oliver's disappearance in the wake of the Undertaking and the destruction of the Glades, Thea took over his role as owner of the nightclub Verdant. She and

"WHY IS IT SO HARD FOR EVERYONE JUST TO TELL THE TRUTH?"

CHARACTER DEVELOPMENT

From party girl to businesswoman to runaway, Thea Queen has evolved a lot, as writer-producer Wendy Mericle reflects. "Initially, Thea was designed to be kind of that wish-fulfilment of a billionaire heiress going to parties and whatnot, but we quickly found that those stories just didn't stick. And we'd initially conceived that Oliver would be dating lots of women and driving fast cars and being a billionaire jerk by day. That did not work in the first season, so we tried to give some of that stuff to Thea, and by season 2 it became clear that to exist on the show, she needed to become a part of Arrow's world, so we moved her into Verdant, we gave her a job, she grew up and graduated from high school, and got involved with Roy. You quickly find where the show lives; Team Arrow and Arrow's lair, that's where this show lives."

After finding out she had been lied to by her brother, her mother, and her boyfriend, a frustrated Thea left Starling City with Malcolm Merlyn, deciding to start her life over.

Roy continued to date, but had constant disagreements over his vigilante actions in the Glades as he tried to fill the void left by the absent Arrow.

Initially angry at her mother for the part she had played in the Undertaking, Thea came to the conclusion that Moira was a victim of circumstances, and that her fear for her family had caused her to help Malcolm. This revelation came on the heels of Thea's own near-death experience after being kidnapped. But Moira's trial provided a shocking revelation for Thea: she had been right about Moira's affair with Malcolm Merlyn, only it had occurred many years earlier.

In "Birds of Prey" (season 2, episode 17), Roy abruptly broke up with Thea, leaving her thoroughly confused. She refused to accept it, and told Roy as much, only to walk in on him making out with another woman at Verdant. Unbeknownst to Thea, Roy had broken up with her at Oliver's behest. Now training as a vigilante with the Arrow, Roy was infected with the highly unstable mirakuru virus, and until he learned to control himself, he was a danger to Thea. After the break-up, Thea bared her soul to Oliver, telling him that everyone in her life was lying to her, and that he was the only one she could trust completely.

On her way home from Verdant, Thea was offered a ride by Slade Wilson in his limousine, which she accepted. Slade then held her for several hours in an undisclosed location in "Deathstroke" (season 2, episode 18), promising to tell her the truth her family had been hiding: that Malcolm Merlyn was her father, and that Oliver knew it.

"Seeing Red" (season 2, episode 20) found Thea continuing to keep distance between herself and her family. After a heart-to-heart talk with Diggle, whom Oliver had assigned to keep Thea safe from Slade Wilson, Thea decided to start over with her family, and had a good talk with Moira and Oliver on the way home. But their time was cut short when Slade Wilson crashed into their limousine and kidnapped them all. Slade pointed a gun at Moira and Thea, forcing Oliver to choose between them in a cruel reflection of Dr. Ivo forcing Oliver to choose between Sara and Shado back on Lian Yu. Oliver refused to choose, so Slade decided to kill Thea. But Moira stood up at the moment, offering herself instead, her final words being, "Thea, I love you. Close your eyes, baby." Slade then ran Moira through with a sword, killing her instantly.

Following her mother's funeral, Thea wanted a change of scenery, and decided to leave Starling City. But she made it only as far as the train station before Slade Wilson's mirakuru army descended upon the city. In "Streets of Fire" (season 2, episode 22) Thea tried to escape the soldiers stalking her, only to be rescued by her father, Malcolm Merlyn, in full Dark Archer garb. Thea responded by grabbing a gun and shooting him.

Malcolm survived the gunshot, and told Thea that he needed her by his side. Thea ran again, this time back to Roy, who was now cured of the mirakuru. Roy promised to leave town with Thea, but she discovered a mask in his backpack, revealing that Roy had been the Arrow's sidekick all along. Frustrated by yet another lie, Thea made the decision to go with Malcolm, joining him in leaving Starling City and her family behind.

After Robert Queen's death, Walter married Moira, proving to be a loyal and loving husband and stepfather.

WALTER STEELE

When Oliver Queen returned home to Starling City after five years on a deserted island, he quickly learned the hard truth that anyone who has been away from home for a while eventually discovers: life goes on. And life had certainly gone on for his mother Moira: following the disappearance and presumed death of her husband Robert when the *Queen's Gambit* sank, she began a relationship with and eventually married the new CEO of Queen Consolidated, the charismatic Walter Steele.

For all appearances, the new family seemed happy; Walter was a loving stepfather who treated Thea well. But Oliver's reappearance shook things up, and before long Walter found himself digging into some of his wife's strange behavior. In "An Innocent Man" (season 1, episode 4), Walter discovered that Moira had salvaged (and was hiding) the remains of the *Queen's Gambit* in a nondescript Starling City warehouse. A confrontation with Moira about it went poorly, and, deciding he could no longer trust his wife, Walter left her. He returned a few weeks later, now working with Queen Consolidated's brightest IT mind, Felicity Smoak, to uncover the depths of Moira's deceptions. Walter discovered the shadowy cabal of business leaders Moira was a part of, which led to

him being kidnapped by one of Malcolm Merlyn's goons and used as leverage in an effort to ensure Moira did not get in the way of his plans.

Walter remained missing until "The Undertaking" (season 1, episode 21), when a laptop stolen from one of the cabal's accountants revealed to Felicity a link to Walter: a $2 million payment to the man who kidnapped him. Felicity went undercover and infiltrated the kidnapper's underground casino, where the criminal claimed that Walter was dead. Saddened by this, Oliver broke the news to his family. Moira immediately confronted Merlyn, who informed her that Walter was actually still alive. Eavesdropping, Oliver overheard them, and hacked Merlyn's phone records to find Walter's location so he could rescue him.

Shortly after his return, Walter revealed to Moira that he knew she had been involved in his kidnapping, and served her with divorce papers, leaving her for good.

Season 2 saw Walter make a surprise return to Moira's side, but he wasn't trying to rekindle their romantic relationship, as Moira hoped. Rather he was assisting a group that wanted Moira to campaign for mayor against Sebastian Blood. His next—and final—appearance at Moira Queen's side was, sadly, at her funeral.

"IF I WAS **TAKING** OUT THE **COMPETITION,** I'D HAVE A LOT OF **KILLING** TO DO IN A VERY **SHORT** AMOUNT OF **TIME."**

LAUREL LANCE

Laurel Lance is the oldest daughter of Quentin and Dinah Lance. As a law student, Laurel was dating Oliver when the *Queen's Gambit* was shipwrecked and lost somewhere in the South Pacific. Her grief doubled when it was revealed that her sister Sara was also on the yacht as Oliver's romantic guest.

When Oliver returned from presumed death five years later, members of the Lance family were the only ones unhappy to see him. Laurel was still angry with him for cheating on her, and blamed him for Sara's death. Oliver soon discovered that Laurel had begun an on-and-off relationship with his best friend, Tommy Merlyn. What's more, she was now working for a legal nonprofit that often came into conflict with the very same people as the ones named on Oliver's list, the powerful corrupt businessmen who were slowly bleeding Starling City dry.

Laurel had several angry confrontations with Oliver in the days following his return from Lian Yu. She also had several angry confrontations with the men on the List, which led to her being saved from danger several times by the new Starling City Vigilante (without realizing that this was Oliver Queen).

In "Damaged" (season 1, episode 5), Laurel shared a kiss with Oliver, admitting that she did still have feelings for him, but that nothing more could ever happen between them. She agreed to represent Oliver after he was arrested and charged with being the Vigilante. Laurel's father, Quentin Lance, who brought the charges against Oliver in the first place, was very upset with this decision, but she told him that he couldn't blame Oliver for Sara's death or for the fact that Dinah had left them afterwards.

After Laurel's nonprofit, CNRI, lost their biggest sponsor in "Legacies" (season 1, episode 6), Tommy offered to host a fundraiser to help offset the

FACT SHEET

Portrayed by: Katie Cassidy

Aliases: none

Current Status: alive

Relationships: Quentin and Dinah Lance (parents), Sara Lance (sister), Oliver Queen (ex-boyfriend), Tommy Merlyn (ex-boyfriend)

Comics History: Dinah Laurel Lance is a DC Comics mainstay as the second Black Canary, ex-wife and longtime crime-fighting partner of Green Arrow.

Laurel and Oliver have a troubled relationship, overshadowed by the latter's selfish actions as a younger man. Despite this, their chemistry is undeniable.

loss. Laurel was initially suspicious, but agreed to it considering how badly they needed the cash infusion. The fundraiser was a success, and Laurel decided that she could perhaps be interested in a long-term relationship with Tommy.

After a firefighter died on the job, his sister approached Laurel about investigating the suspicious nature of the fire. Laurel went to her father, who refused to help because the official ruling said there was nothing suspicious about it. Undaunted, Laurel stole the phone that provided Quentin a direct line to the Hood. After she helped prove that the death was, in fact, a murder, Quentin told Laurel to keep the phone, saying she'd find a better use for it than he would. Laurel turned to the Hood again in "Betrayal" (season 1, episode 13), asking for his help when a dangerous criminal, Cyrus Vanch, was released from prison. When the Hood called to set up a meeting, Laurel left a date with Tommy to meet him on a rooftop, not realizing that Quentin was tracking the call in an attempt to capture the Hood. This incident set off a chain of resentment: Tommy was upset with Laurel for contacting the Hood, Laurel was angry at Tommy for being upset about her putting her own life in danger, and Laurel was furious with her father for using her as bait. When the dust settled, Laurel was kidnapped by Vanch, but she was rescued by her father and the Hood. The

latter saw how much danger he was putting her in, and told her that he would stay away from her.

Dinah Lance returned to Starling City in "Dead to Rights" (season 1, episode 16), hoping to convince Laurel to share her belief that Sara was still alive. Laurel set up a breakfast with her parents, hoping to convince Quentin to help her mother investigate whether or not Sara had survived so they could prove to her that Sara really was dead. Ultimately, Laurel was able to prove that the girl in the photo Dinah believed to be Sara was, in fact, someone else entirely.

When Laurel and Tommy took refuge at Queen Mansion in "Home Invasion" (season 1, episode 20) after Laurel angered a dangerous criminal, Edward Rasmus, Tommy witnessed just how strong a bond remained between Oliver and Laurel. He came to the conclusion that if she ever had to choose between them, Laurel would pick Oliver, especially now that Tommy knew Oliver was actually the Hood, whom Laurel admired. Choosing to save himself the heartbreak later, Tommy broke up with Laurel, lying when he said he wasn't ready for a relationship.

A few days later, Laurel went to Tommy, saying that she still loved him and believed that he still loved her; Tommy responded that Oliver was still in love with her, and that she should be with him instead. Laurel then

LOVE TRIANGLE

It's clear that Laurel Lance is the love of Oliver Queen's life, but they've had to surmount many obstacles in their relationship, and one unexpected obstacle in particular could prove stronger than Oliver's love for Laurel—his feelings for Felicity Smoak. "From day one in the writer's room, Sara was on the boat with Oliver. This was a huge betrayal of Laurel, and we knew that she was alive and that eventually we were going to reveal that," shares writer-producer Wendy Mericle. "It created a great mystery. It was just a better story to talk about the disappearance of her sister and Oliver's betrayal, and it spoke a lot to defining Oliver's character before the island, which was a spoiled rich kid who cheats on his girlfriend with her sister. That's hitting a low watermark morally.

"The relationship element is that you don't want to get them together too soon; you always want problems between them to prevent that from happening. That said, while we still are honoring the comic-book element of Laurel and Oliver being lifelong lovers and that being the primary relationship, with the introduction of Felicity, that part is shifting...

"I couldn't tell you right now whether Felicity will be the love of Oliver's life or if it will be Laurel," Mericle muses. "We've ended up with a bit of a triangle, and that was just one of those serendipitous pure luck situations where we cast a day player from Vancouver to play Felicity and she turned out to be this amazing find. We started writing to her. From a storytelling perspective, we have a triangle that could go on for many, many seasons. And it has changed how we originally conceived of the Oliver/Laurel story."

"LAUREL, IF YOU **WANNA** HAVE **DINNER**, OR COFFEE, I DON'T KNOW... **CALL ME**...
I DON'T WANT TO BE ON AN **ISLAND** ANYMORE."

Laurel becomes increasingly caught up in Oliver's fight against Starling City's villains, which tests her bravery and resilience.

went to Oliver, hoping that he would tell Tommy he didn't love her. But Oliver couldn't do that, saying he had too many lies in his life already. Oliver and Laurel ended up sleeping together, which Tommy witnessed from the street below, having come to reconcile with Laurel.

Laurel returned to the Glades over Oliver's objections on the night Malcolm Merlyn's Undertaking destroyed the neighborhood, desperate to save some valuable client files from her office. She was trapped amongst some falling rubble when the building collapsed. The Arrow didn't arrive in time to save her, but Tommy did. He managed to get her out, but was killed by more debris as he did so.

Having gotten used to the Arrow always having her back, Laurel blamed him for not being there to save Tommy. Working for the District Attorney's (DA) office following the destruction of CNRI, she vowed to bring the Hood to justice for all of his crimes. In "Broken Dolls" (season 2, episode 3), Laurel is kidnapped by the serial killer her father is hunting, the Dollmaker, who attempted to turn her into a lifelike—but very dead—doll, making Quentin watch all the while. The Arrow arrived just in time and saved her life, forcing Laurel to realize that her anger was actually misplaced guilt, and that the person she really blamed for Tommy's death was herself. To cope with all of this, as well as the host of traumatic events in

her life over the previous five years, Laurel began to drink heavily, mixing alcohol with antidepressants.

Laurel was assigned to the Moira Queen murder case as Oliver's mother went on trial for her role in planning the Undertaking. When Assistant District Attorney (ADA) Adam Donner collapsed from Vertigo poisoning, Laurel was appointed lead prosecutor. While reviewing the notes for the case, she discovered what Donner had been calling his trump card—the fact that Moira had once had an affair with the Undertaking's mastermind, Malcolm Merlyn. After revealing this fact in her cross-examination, Laurel tried to avoid Oliver outside the courtroom, wracked with guilt over her courtroom performance. But despite Laurel's best efforts, Moira was found innocent of all charges, thanks to some behind-the-scenes manipulation from Malcolm Merlyn himself, who was believed to have died during the Undertaking.

Laurel was suspicious of the too-good-to-be-true city council member (and mayoral candidate) Sebastian Blood, and began to investigate him in "Blast Radius" (season 2, episode 10). Her snooping led her to a psychiatric institution and Maya Resik, a woman she believed to be Blood's aunt but who was actually his mother. From Resik, Laurel learned a horrible truth: Sebastian had murdered his father as a child, and that his mother was blamed and placed in a mental institution.

Confident, intelligent, and principled, Laurel is dedicated to fighting on behalf of Starling City's disadvantaged.

Feeling the pressure of Laurel's investigation, Blood had Laurel's apartment ransacked; when the police arrived, they found her in illegal possession of prescription drugs and promptly arrested her. Upon her release, she was kidnapped (again!) by one of Blood's agents. The Arrow came to rescue her from a masked captor, but it was Laurel that shot and killed the man, believing him to be Blood. It was actually corrupt police officer Daily. As a result of her seemingly false accusations against the future mayor, together with her drug use, Laurel was fired by ADA Donner and spiraled deeper into her addictions.

In "Heir to the Demon" (season 2, episode 13), Dinah Lance was kidnapped in order to force Sara Lance (now revealed to have survived the sinking of the *Queen's Gambit* and in town aiding Oliver in his vigilante war) to rejoin the League of Assassins and return to their headquarters at Nanda Parbat. The Lance family was finally reunited after Dinah's rescue—but Laurel took the happy moment as an opportunity to blame Sara for every bad thing that had happened to her over the last six years.

After a tense family dinner in "Time of Death" (season 2, episode 14), Oliver told Laurel he was done with her, and that he could not be her friend anymore unless she got her act together. This seemed to have the desired effect, and Laurel made the decision to start attending Alcoholics Anonymous meetings with her father. Laurel got her job back at the DA's office after ADA Donner's spectacularly botched attempt at arresting Helena Bertinelli in "Birds of Prey" (season 2, episode 17) left Donner himself fired, and Laurel in a position to blackmail DA Spencer by threatening to go public with Donner's actions unless she was reinstated.

Slade Wilson paid a visit to Laurel in "Deathstroke" (season 2, episode 18) and revealed Oliver's true identity as the Hood. But rather than upsetting her, this only strengthened her feelings for Oliver, and when Laurel saw a number of wounds on her sister soon thereafter, she quickly realized that Sara was the Canary.

"I KNOW A GUILTY MAN WHEN I SEE ONE."

QUENTIN LANCE

Quentin Lance is an officer with the Starling City Police Department. He and his ex-wife Dinah Lance have two daughters, Laurel and Sara. The family was devastated five years before *Arrow* started when Sara was lost at sea and presumed dead in the wake of the *Queen's Gambit* shipwreck in the South Pacific. Quentin turned to alcohol and his job to help him cope with the loss, soon becoming an alcoholic. This was the final straw for Dinah, who promptly divorced him and moved to Central City.

About a month after Sara disappeared, Starling City was besieged by a serial killer known as the Dollmaker (real name Barton Mathis), who kidnapped and murdered young girls. All the victims reminded Quentin of Sara, and he came dangerously close to losing his grip on things as the body count mounted. But Quentin held on, and was able to arrest and incarcerate the Dollmaker before he collected any more victims.

The return of Oliver Queen hit Quentin pretty hard, as Oliver provided him with a living, breathing reminder (and target for blame) of all the things the Lance family had lost. Around the same time, a mysterious hooded vigilante began targeting the rich and powerful of Starling City, and Quentin made it his personal mission to arrest him, not realizing that the Hood and Oliver Queen were one and the same.

FACT SHEET

Portrayed by: Paul Blackthorne

Aliases: none

Current Status: alive

Relationships: Dinah Lance (wife, divorced), Laurel Lance (daughter), Sara Lance (daughter)

Comics History: Quentin Larry Lance is an *Arrow* original character, and has yet to make an appearance in the comics. Larry Lance, however, was a police detective married to Dinah Lance, the original Black Canary. Their daughter, Dinah Laurel Lance, became the second Black Canary.

Quentin takes his job as a police officer seriously. At first he actively tried to arrest the Vigilante, but after the destruction of the Glades he came to recognize him as a force for good in Starling City.

Quentin became obsessed with the Hood, believing that the Hood's outside-the-law methods for fighting crime made him as much of a criminal as the men he had vowed to stop. He drafted fellow detective McKenna Hall into his crusade after seeing she was of a similar mind when it came to vigilante justice.

When Laurel was kidnapped by ex-con Cyrus Vanch in "Betrayal" (season 1, episode 13), Quentin actually teamed up with the Hood to rescue her. As Vance was subdued, Quentin went to kill him but was stopped by the Hood, who reminded Quentin that he was a cop, not a killer, and that he should arrest him instead.

Dinah Lance returned to Starling City in "Salvation" (season 1, episode 18), claiming to have photographic evidence that Sara was still alive. Quentin wanted desperately to believe her, but Laurel soon proved that the picture was of another woman.

Quentin arrested Queen Consolidated IT staffer Felicity Smoak in "Sacrifice" (season 1, episode 23) based on his suspicions that she was working with the Hood. While he was interrogating her, Quentin received a call from the Hood telling him that the Glades was about to be destroyed, thanks to the Undertaking. At Felicity's urging, Quentin went to his superiors with the information, even though he knew that talking to the

Hood without arresting him on sight could damage his career. But his bosses did nothing with the information, leaving Quentin to work side by side with the Hood and his partners to deactivate one of the Markov devices Merlyn was using to level the Glades.

As the dust settled across Starling City following the Undertaking, Quentin was demoted from detective back to a regular police officer. Soon thereafter, he learned that Barton Mathis (along with countless others) had escaped from Iron Heights prison during the Undertaking. In "Broken Dolls" (season 2, episode 3) Mathis began killing young women once again in a gruesome fashion. In order to stop him, Quentin worked with the Arrow and Felicity to track the killer down, but Quentin himself was captured and forced to watch as Mathis attempted to kill Laurel by injecting liquid plastic into her bloodstream, turning her into a doll. This sick plan was foiled by the Arrow and his new ally, the Canary, a young woman who seemed somehow familiar to Quentin.

The Canary was unmasked in "League of Assassins" (season 2, episode 5) as Sara Lance—who was not dead after all, but alive and well fighting crime in Starling City. A mysterious group of assassins arrived in town with orders to bring Sara back to Nanda Parbat, the headquarters of the League of Assassins, of which she had been a part. When she refused, they threatened to kill her

LANCE VS ARROW

"We wanted to explore the tension between what Oliver was doing and what the police were doing," notes writer-producer Wendy Mericle, regarding the relationship between the Arrow and Detective Quentin Lance. "In the beginning, Starling was a lot like Gotham at its worst in that the criminals were running amok and the police were powerless to do anything, and it was only through the Arrow that they were even able to get a foothold at all in terms of taming the Glades and stopping Malcolm in season 1. In the beginning, Lance didn't like him; Indeed he hated the Arrow... for a couple of reasons: one, he was working outside the law; two, he was making them look bad. Being a detective is very much in Lance's blood; it's very much who he is. He believes in the law and that the law is the only way he knows how to regulate his own behavior. I think he has a lot of the same tendencies that

the Arrow does; he has no tolerance for these criminals, he understands what the Arrow's trying to do, and wishes he could do it, but knows that he can't."

Still, it's not until the Arrow makes the decision not to kill that Quentin becomes open to the notion of allying with him. "He's not in favor of one man being judge, jury, and executioner," Mericle agrees. "Once he makes that turn, he's willing to risk everything because he recognizes that the Arrow is doing things in the city that the police can't and that are absolutely necessary for the greater good. [Their relationship] kind of has a father-son overtone to it. He doesn't know that the Arrow is Oliver, the Arrow knows that Lance is the father of the love of his life, so it has a lot of interesting layers. Those scenes are sometimes the hardest to write because you're dealing with so many different character elements."

Although no longer a young man, Lance is never afraid to throw himself into the action when necessary.

family. In order to keep Quentin safe, Sara revealed herself to him and brought him to her clock-tower hideaway. After the Lances worked together with the Arrow to fight off the assassins once more, Sara realized that her family would be in danger as long as she remained in Starling City, and decided to leave. But before doing so, she extracted a promise from Quentin to tell neither Laurel nor her mother that she was still alive, believing that a lack of awareness would help keep them safe from the League of Assassins.

Before long, Sara returned to Starling City, followed in short order by Nyssa al Ghūl, one of the League's top assassins, in "Heir to the Demon" (season 2, episode 13). This time, the League kidnapped Dinah Lance,

Lance was overjoyed when reunited with his daughter Sara, who he thought had drowned over five years before.

threatening to kill her if Sara did not return to Nanda Parbat. Eager to end this danger to her family for good, Sara agreed to exchange her mother for herself, before revealing that she had already ingested a slow-acting, deadly poison. The Arrow was able to save Sara with medicinal herbs he brought back from Lian Yu, and Nyssa, touched by the ultimate sacrifice Sara was willing to make, released Sara from her League obligations once and for all. The Lance family was finally reunited; Quentin and Dinah were still divorced, but happier than they had been in years. Unfortunately, Laurel, now in a near-constant haze brought on by alcohol and pills, was having none of it, and raged at Sara that her only sister was the cause of every terrible thing that had happened to her in the past few years. Seeing signs of his own behavior in his daughter, Quentin badgered her until she agreed to attend an Alcoholics Anonymous meeting with him.

In "Deathstroke" (season 2, episode 18), Quentin arrested Slade Wilson at the Arrow's request for the kidnapping of Thea Queen, but was later forced to release him because of a lack of evidence. After this embarrassment to the department, Quentin himself was arrested and tossed in jail for knowingly aiding and abetting the vigilante Arrow. While in prison, Quentin was assaulted by another inmate who blamed the detective for the arrest that landed him in jail. Laurel visited Quentin in the prison hospital, intending to let him know that she now knew the Arrow's secret identity,

but he stopped her before she could tell him, since he now firmly believed in the Arrow's mission, and that given the vigilante's importance to the people of Starling City, a little jail time was the least he could do to help the Arrow out.

After Laurel pulled some strings at the DA's office to get him released from jail, Quentin got another bit of good news: in the aftermath of Slade Wilson's mirakuru army assault on the city, he was reinstated to the rank of detective to help coordinate the city's defense. Quentin and his fellow officers fought valiantly, and with the help of both Team Arrow and Sara's friends from the League of Assassins, they were able to stop Slade's army.

"IT'S THE ARROW THAT MATTERS. THE MAN UNDER THE HOOD ISN'T IMPORTANT."

"WE'RE BOTH GHOSTS. WE DIED ON THAT ISLAND."

SARA LANCE

Sara Lance is the daughter of Quentin and Dinah Lance, and the younger sister of Laurel Lance. While in high school, Sara was bullied after stealing one of her classmate's boyfriends; this led to behavior issues and poor grades, which in turn prompted her father, a police detective, to teach Sara and her sister how to defend themselves.

As young women, the Lance sisters met a pair of super-rich, super-cute playboys: Oliver Queen and Tommy Merlyn. Sara developed a crush on Oliver but never acted on it, and before long it was too late as Oliver and Laurel began dating. Things got pretty serious between Oliver and Laurel, who started talking about moving in together. This freaked Oliver out, and he began sleeping with Sara. Oliver even went so far as to invite Sara to come along on a Pacific cruise aboard his family's yacht, the *Queen's Gambit*.

The trip ended in tragedy, however, as Malcolm Merlyn sabotaged the boat, sinking it in an effort to kill Oliver's father, Robert Queen. Oliver managed to survive, washing ashore on the seemingly deserted island of Lian Yu. But Sara was not so fortunate, and Oliver presumed that she had drowned.

However, Sara was not dead; she floated along on a piece of wreckage before being found and rescued by another boat: the *Amazo*. The ship was a floating chamber of horrors, and the personal laboratory for mad scientist Dr. Anthony Ivo, a self-styled savior of the human race. Rather than toss Sara in a cell with his other human test subjects, Ivo enlisted Sara's help in his hunt for a legendary Japanese serum called mirakuru, which enhanced the body's strength, senses, and cell regeneration. She agreed, and spent the next year helping Ivo torture and experiment upon the other prisoners on the boat.

A year later, Sara was jolted out of her nightmare life by the arrival of a newcomer aboard the *Amazo*: Oliver Queen. Before long, Sara was helping Oliver and his friends from Lian Yu, Slade Wilson, and Shado, in their conflict with Ivo. After finding the mirakuru and dosing Slade with it in an effort to heal his combat injuries, Oliver and the women were taken captive by Ivo's men, and the doctor forced Oliver to choose between Shado and Sara—one of them would live, and one would die, and the choice was Oliver's. He chose Sara, but it was just another black mark on her soul when Ivo killed Shado in her place.

In their final battle with Ivo, Oliver and Sara were separated once more when a torpedo blast tore a hole through the *Amazo* and Sara was washed away. Oliver was certain she was dead this time, but once again he was wrong. This time, Sara was found by Nyssa al Ghūl,

"WHAT I AM... IS IRREDEEMABLE"

Sara's return caused some mixed emotions in the Lance household, after having been thought dead for so long.

daughter of Rā's al Ghūl of the feared League of Assassins. She was nursed back to health in Nanda Parbat, where she entered into a romantic relationship with Nyssa and swore her allegiance to the League, becoming an assassin.

Following the Undertaking in Starling City, Sara left Nanda Parbat and returned home to make sure her family was safe. This visit would also give her a chance to see first-hand the growing legend of the Starling City vigilante known as the Hood. Sara hadn't been in town long before she reintroduced herself in a way that would make Oliver proud: beating up a group of men who had been attacking a woman. Wearing black leather and a blonde wig that hid her, um, blonde hair (ingenious!),

Sara soon attracted the attention of the Hood, although he had yet to realize her true identity. She was also noticed by one of Rā's al Ghūl's assassins, who came to Starling City to force her to return to Nanda Parbat; Sara killed him for his troubles.

Felicity Smoak was the first to make the connection between the new female vigilante and Sara Lance; following the patterns in the Canary's appearances, it became obvious that she was shadowing Laurel. Oliver used this information to catch her, and was shocked to learn that Sara was alive.

The Arrow and the Canary began teaming up to fight crime regularly, and Oliver and Sara began teaming up once more as well, as Sara secretly moved into the Queen Mansion. But their peaceful existence was short-lived, as another League Assassin arrived to return Sara to Rā's al Ghūl. This visitor prompted Sara to reveal her time with the League to Oliver. In order to protect her family from the League, Sara decided to reveal herself to her father as well, telling him everything (except Oliver's identity as the Arrow). In order to keep her family safe, Sara ultimately decided to leave Starling City and draw the assassins away with her, but not before forcing her father to promise not to tell Laurel that she was still alive.

Sara returned to Starling City after a phone call from Oliver explaining that Laurel needed her sister's help with her growing chemical dependencies. Sara visited Laurel in her apartment (a visit that a drug-addled Laurel would pass off as a hallucination), but before she could leave Starling City, Sara was once more confronted by the League, this time in the form of her former lover Nyssa al Ghūl. Nyssa proceeded to kidnap Dinah Lance, threatening to kill Sara's mother if Sara did not return to the League within 24 hours. Sara came to the conclusion that the only way to end the League's obsession with getting her back would be to end her own life; to that end, she handed herself over to Nyssa, but not before ingesting a slow-acting poison. Oliver used a herbal remedy he brought back from Lian Yu to save Sara, and Nyssa, deeply moved by Sara's act of self-sacrifice, released her from her obligations to the League. Sara then had a tearful reunion with her family, who were all glad to see her alive once more—except for Laurel, who blamed her sister for everything that had gone wrong in her life over the last six years.

After Roy Harper was driven insane by the mirakuru serum in "Seeing Red" (season 2, episode 20), Sara, remembering what had happened to Slade Wilson, decided that the only way to stop Roy would be to kill him. Oliver stopped her before she was able to kill Roy, and Sara confessed to him that she didn't truly want to finish Roy, but that the League of Assassins had reprogrammed her mind. Telling Oliver that he needed someone who could still see the good in things, Sara broke up with him and left Starling City once more.

She returned during the rampage of Slade Wilson's mirakuru army in the season 2 finale, "Unthinkable" (season 2, episode 23). But she didn't return alone: Sara brought Nyssa al Ghūl and a cadre of League Assassins to help even the odds against Slade. Despite Oliver's initial misgivings, the Assassins were a much-needed force, and helped turn back the tide of Slade's men. But their help came at a cost: Sara returned to Nanda Parbat with Nyssa the very next morning, to rejoin the League of Assassins and leave Starling City and her family behind.

"YOU **DON'T KNOW** ABOUT ME. ABOUT **WHO I AM**, AND WHO I'VE **BECOME.**"

DINAH LANCE

Dinah Lance is the estranged wife of Starling City police officer Quentin Lance; together, they have two daughters, Laurel and Sara.

Following Sara's disappearance and presumed death from the shipwreck of the *Queen's Gambit*, Quentin began to drink heavily, and the Lances' marriage disintegrated as Dinah left town. She returned late in the first season with a photograph, which she shared with both Quentin and Laurel. It showed a blonde woman somewhere in China whom Dinah believed to be Sara. Quentin, desperate to reunite his family, believed her, but Laurel was skeptical, eventually identifying the woman and proving that she was not Sara after all.

Dinah returned in "Heir to the Demon" (season 2, episode 13), only to be kidnapped by Nyssa Al Ghūl, who threatened to kill Dinah unless Sara agreed to return to Nanda Parbat within 24 hours. Sara agreed in order to save her mother, but drank snake venom in a self-sacrifice meant to keep her from returning to the League of Assassins. The Arrow saved Sara at the last second with an antidote, and Nyssa, shaken by Sara's love for her mother and unquestionable desire to leave the assassin life behind, released Sara from her obligations to the League of Assassins.

Dinah was overjoyed to find Sara still alive, and Quentin remained hopeful that his family could be reunited once more. But Dinah revealed that she had a boyfriend in Central City and had no intention of coming back to Quentin and Starling City.

FACT SHEET

Portrayed by: Alex Kingston

Aliases: none

Current Status: alive

Relationships: Quentin Lance (ex-husband), Laurel Lance (daughter), Sara Lance (daughter)

Comics History: Dinah Lance is one of the comics' top heroines, fighting crime as the Black Canary for two generations. The original Dinah Lance first appeared in *Flash Comics* #86 in 1947. Her daughter, Dinah Laurel Lance, debuted in *Justice League of America* #75 in 1969.

FACT SHEET

Portrayed by: David Ramsey
Aliases: none
Current Status: alive
Relationships: Lyla Michaels (ex-wife, current girlfriend); Andy Diggle (brother, deceased), Carly Diggle (sister-in-law, former girlfriend), Andrew Diggle (nephew), Team Arrow

Comics History: John Diggle was created for *Arrow*, but crossed over into the comics with his 2013 appearance in *Green Arrow* #24. His character in the comics is nearly identical to the one from the show.

JOHN DIGGLE

John Diggle is a former Army special forces soldier who was brought into Oliver Queen's life by his mother Moira as a one-man protection detail following the attempted kidnapping of Oliver upon his return from five years on a deserted island. But Diggle quickly became more than that; he discovered Oliver's secret vigilante life as the Hood and became first a trusted advisor, then an active partner in Oliver's war against crime and corruption.

Diggle did three tours in Afghanistan. During his second tour his unit was ambushed, and everyone but Diggle was killed. This experience gave him survivor's guilt, which rears its head from time to time. Diggle also met and married fellow soldier Lyla Michaels in Afghanistan, but the marriage couldn't handle the transition to peace upon their return stateside, and it soon fell apart.

Diggle spent most of his first few days working for the Queens trying to find Oliver whenever he vanished, as was often the case. Oliver got more and more creative in his escapes so he could head out as the Starling City Vigilante.

Diggle had a brother named Andy, who was shot and killed by Deadshot while working as a bodyguard. In "Lone Gunmen" (season 1, episode 3), Diggle himself was shot by Deadshot, and Oliver had no choice but to take him to his hideaway in the old Queen Consolidated foundry to heal up. When Diggle awoke, he learned just where Oliver disappeared to every night. His initial reaction was to quit on the spot, as he did not approve of the lethal means the Vigilante employed to combat Starling City corruption, but he reconsidered and signed back on, just in time to see Oliver arrested and charged with being the Vigilante. With Oliver under house arrest, Diggle donned the hood himself to stop an arms dealer, saving Oliver from prison in the process.

In "Dead to Rights" (season 1, episode 16) Diggle and Oliver learn that Deadshot is still alive after an assassin nearly kills Malcolm Merlyn using curare-tipped bullets, which are a Deadshot trademark. They unveil a plan to take down Deadshot in "Home Invasion" (season 1, episode 20), unaware that the potential client Deadshot was returning to Starling to meet was actually an A.R.G.U.S. sting operation. When Diggle got to the mall where the meet was to take place, he found it swarming with A.R.G.U.S. agents, including his ex-wife Lyla. Deadshot was also waiting, and opened fire from a balcony. Diggle was able to save Lyla, then squared off against Deadshot, at which point both men swore to kill one another before Deadshot made another getaway. The Hood arrived too late to stop Deadshot's escape, angering Diggle so much that he quit the team.

"I'M **NOT** THE KIND OF **MAN** YOU WANT TO TAKE FOR A **FOOL**, MR. **QUEEN**."

"SUPER STRENGTH? LIKES BLOOD? PLEASE DON'T TELL ME WE'RE STARTING TO BELIEVE IN VAMPIRES."

A former special forces soldier, John Diggle is no stranger to conflict, and proves to be highly competent in backing up the Arrow.

Diggle returned in "The Undertaking" (season 1, episode 21), after Oliver apologized. Oliver then told Diggle about Moira Queen's involvement in the Undertaking, saying he would need all the help he could get to stop it. Diggle posed as the Vigilante once more, beating Oliver in front of Moira in order to get her to give up information on Malcolm Merlyn's plan. Diggle then rescued Oliver from captivity at the hands of Malcolm Merlyn and, together with Felicity, the team discovered that the earthquake device was located in a Starling City subway tunnel. Diggle and Oliver went after the Dark Archer, but Diggle was wounded, making it up a staircase just in time to see Oliver kill Malcolm Merlyn. Just then, a previously unknown second device went off, destroying the Glades.

Five months after the Undertaking, Diggle and Felicity traveled to Lian Yu to see Oliver, who had returned there in a funk over the way the Undertaking played out. They convinced him to return home to Starling City. A short while later, Diggle headed to Russia in "Keep Your Enemies Closer" (season 2, episode 6) to find Lyla, who had disappeared on an undercover operation inside a Russian gulag. Oliver used his *bratva* (Russian mafia) connections

to get Diggle arrested and shipped to the same prison, where he found Deadshot, the reason for Lyla's mission in the first place. With Deadshot's help, Diggle freed Lyla, and in exchange for his own freedom, Deadshot informed Diggle that he had been hired by an organization called H.I.V.E. to kill Andy Diggle. Upon their return to the States, Diggle and Lyla rekindled their romance.

Diggle was recruited by Lyla's A.R.G.U.S. boss, Amanda Waller, in "Suicide Squad" (season 2, episode 16) to lead a team of convicts, including Deadshot, to destroy nerve gas in the possession of known terrorist Gholem Qadeer. Once again, Diggle kept Deadshot alive, convincing the assassin not to sacrifice himself for the mission as a drone strike bore down on Qadeer's mansion to destroy the nerve gas.

As Slade Wilson's mirakuru army rampaged through Starling City in "Streets of Fire" (season 2, episode 22), Diggle and Lyla freed Deadshot from an A.R.G.U.S. prison and partnered with him to force Waller to call off another drone strike, this one targeting Starling City itself. Waller agreed, in an act of self-preservation, but not before dropping a bombshell on Diggle: Lyla was pregnant, and he was going to be a father.

"SECRETS HAVE **WEIGHT. THE MORE** YOU **KEEP,** THE **HARDER** IT IS TO **KEEP MOVING."**

DIGGIN' THE ORIGIN

"Whenever possible, we try to draw from the comics," notes executive producer Marc Guggenheim. However, the show's creators did not find a character in Green Arrow comics that perfectly fit their needs, and the supporting role was ultimately filled with the original character John Diggle. "From the comics, there's obviously Roy Harper as Speedy and there's Dinah Lance, who's Black Canary, but both of those are Super Heroes. In terms of non-Super Hero supporting cast, Green Arrow doesn't have a Jimmy Olsen, he doesn't have an Alfred. We created Diggle mainly so that Arrow would have a confidant and a sidekick that we could drive story through."

"IF YOU BELIEVE IN SOMETHING, HOW CAN IT BE WRONG?"

CARLY DIGGLE

FACT SHEET

Portrayed by: Christie Laing
Aliases: none
Current Status: alive
Relationships: Andy Diggle (husband, deceased), Andrew Diggle (son), John Diggle (brother-in-law, ex-boyfriend)

Comics History: Carly Diggle has yet to appear in the comics.

Carly Diggle is the widow of Andy Diggle (younger brother of John Diggle), who was killed by Deadshot at some point before *Arrow* began. Carly works as a server at a Big Belly Burger restaurant in downtown Starling City, where her brother-in-law and Oliver Queen often stopped by for late-night meals in season 1. It was clear from her first appearance that she and John had romantic feelings for one another, and were only holding back on acting on those feelings out of respect for Andy's memory.

In "Trust but Verify" (season 1, episode 11) Carly was kidnapped by John's old commanding officer Ted Gaynor in an attempt to force John to help him with a bank heist, but the Hood and Diggle's grenade launcher took care of that threat. John and Carly began dating, but it didn't last. Between the end of season 1 and the start of season 2 they broke up over John's dangerous obsession with tracking down his brother's murderer.

FELICITY SMOAK

Felicity Megan Smoak grew up in Las Vegas the daughter of a single mother who worked as a cocktail waitress. Interested in computers from a young age, she built her first at the age of seven. The fear of ending up a waitress like her mother drove Felicity to go to college, and then to move a thousand miles away to Starling City for a job in the Queen Consolidated IT department.

In "An Innocent Man" (season 1, episode 4) Felicity was summoned to the office of CEO Walter Steele, leading her to assume she was about to be fired. Instead, Walter gave her an assignment to research the details of one of Moira Queen's transactions. This research ultimately led Felicity to uncover details of the Undertaking, Malcolm Merlyn's criminal conspiracy to destroy the Glades. Around the same time, Felicity also began working on some special assignments for Oliver Queen, not yet realizing that this extracurricular research was actually being done for the Vigilante, Oliver's alter ego.

In "The Odyssey" (season 1, episode 14) Felicity climbed into her car late one night after work and found a man in the back seat wearing a hood and suffering from a gunshot wound: Oliver Queen. At that point, everything became "so unbelievably clear" for Felicity: the odd research requests, the strange hours, the physical ailments. Oliver Queen was the Hood.

Oliver asked Felicity to drive him to the Foundry, where she and John Diggle operated on Oliver and managed to stop the bleeding. Realizing how much she had helped with the Hood's crusade already, Felicity agreed to stay on and help until Walter Steele was found (he had mysteriously disappeared a short while prior), after which

FACT SHEET

Portrayed by: Emily Bett Rickards

Aliases: none

Current Status: alive

Relationships: Team Arrow

Comics History: Felicity Smoak made her DC Comics debut in 1984 as a supporting character in the pages of *Firestorm*. Other than the name and her acumen with computers, there are not many similarities between the television and print iterations of the character. In the comics, Felicity Smoak was the manager of a New York computer software firm, and the stepmother of Ronnie Raymond, Firestorm's secret identity.

From computer hacking to electronics, Felicity's technical expertise is indispensable for Team Arrow.

she planned to return to her simpler life as a corporate IT worker.

But Felicity stuck around even after Walter was rescued by the Hood, working with Oliver and Diggle to uncover just what exactly the Undertaking was, and the role Moira Queen had in planning and executing it. Following the threads of the case, Felicity uncovered Unidac Industries, a Queen subsidiary that specialized in seismic infringement. When the Dark Archer massacred scientists in a Unidac lab, the group realized that he was working for Malcolm Merlyn to tie up loose ends before the Undertaking, and that they did not have much time left to stop him.

In "Sacrifice" (season 1, episode 23) Felicity was arrested by Quentin Lance and charged with aiding and abetting the Vigilante after a computer trail of the Hood's activities traced back to her desk at work. But Felicity was able to convince Lance that the Hood was more of a hero than the detective gave him credit for, considering all that he had sacrificed for Starling City. At the Hood's behest, Felicity and Lance worked together to disarm Malcolm Merlyn's earthquake machine, only to tragically learn that there was a second device hidden elsewhere in the Glades. They watched helplessly as the east side of the neighborhood was reduced to rubble.

A few months after the Undertaking, Felicity and Diggle traveled to Lian Yu to bring Oliver back to Starling City. The three of them returned just in time to stop a hostile takeover of Queen Consolidated. With Oliver now more involved with the day-to-day operations of the company, he made Felicity his executive assistant, making it easier to explain the work she was doing for him.

Felicity went into the field to help catch the "Dollmaker" (season 2, episode 3), acting as bait by going from store to store buying the same lotion all of his victims used. She was attacked by the killer and injured before the Arrow arrivedand chased him off.

Felicity was the first one to notice the pattern surrounding the new female vigilante that had arrived in Starling City not long after Oliver returned; so far, she had only appeared to help the Arrow in locations where Laurel Lance was also nearby, which led Felicity to believe she wasn't actually following Oliver, but Laurel. Using this information, Oliver was able to trap the woman and unmask her, revealing her to be the seemingly long-dead Sara Lance, who had been presumed drowned.

Felicity traveled to Russia with Oliver, Diggle, and Queen Consolidated co-CEO Isabel Rochev in "Keep Your Enemies Closer" (season 2, episode 6). After Oliver and Isabel slept together one night, Felicity confronted Oliver about it, visibly upset, and implied that she had feelings

"YOU COULD HAVE **CALLED** BEFORE YOU INVITED **SEVEN ASSASSINS** INTO OUR **LAIR.**"

As Oliver gets to know Felicity better, he comes to see her as much more than a friend, eventually falling in love.

for him. Oliver told her that sleeping with Isabel didn't mean anything to him, and furthermore, that he could never be involved with someone he cared about because of the dangers and complications of the vigilante lifestyle, implying that he also had feelings for Felicity but did not want to act upon them.

Felicity met Barry Allen for the first time in "The Scientist" (season 2, episode 8), as the Central City police technician traveled to Starling City to investigate a break-in at one of the Queen Consolidated Applied Science divisions. There was a clear attraction between the two throughout Barry's visit, and when the Arrow fell prey to an unknown poison, Felicity called Barry to help save him, thus revealing Oliver's secret life to yet another person. After Barry returned to Central City, he gave Felicity a call to say that if she ever felt like going on a date with someone who wasn't Oliver Queen, then that someone (meaning him, of course) wouldn't be late for that date. Before Felicity could take him up on that offer, Barry was struck by lightning in a freak accident in his lab, which put him in a coma.

In "Heir to the Demon" (season 2, episode 13), Felicity discovered that Thea Queen, Oliver's sister, was not truly Robert Queen's daughter, but the child of Moira Queen and Malcolm Merlyn. When she confronted Moira about this, Moira used Felicity's feelings for Oliver against her, saying that if Felicity told him, Oliver may hate Moira but he would blame Felicity. Thusly manipulated, Felicity decided not to tell Oliver, but ultimately couldn't keep the secret and told him anyway, an act that led to massive shockwaves throughout the Queen family.

After Moira was murdered by Slade Wilson in "Seeing Red" (season 2, episode 20), Felicity and Diggle enlisted the help of A.R.G.U.S. head honcho Amanda Waller to track down the missing Oliver, who had vanished following his mother's death. When Slade's army of mirakuru-enhanced soldiers rampaged across the city a few days later, Felicity went into the field once more, working with Diggle to stop Isabel Rochev; Felicity ran over Isabel with their van to save Diggle's life. She was also there for Oliver's final showdown with Slade, who kidnapped her after being duped into believing she was Oliver's one true love, the woman he cared more about than any other. This allowed her to get close enough to inject Slade with the mirakuru cure, which returned him to mere mortal status, able to be defeated by the Arrow.

"I JUST **HACKED** A **FEDERAL AGENCY**. KIND OF MAKES ME A **CYBER-TERRORIST**, WHICH IS **BAD**."

FACT SHEET

Portrayed by: Colin Donnell
Aliases: none
Current Status: deceased
Relationships: Malcolm Merlyn (father), Rebecca Merlyn (mother, deceased), Thea Queen (half-sister), Laurel Lance (ex-girlfriend)

Comics History: Tommy Merlyn debuted in the comics in November 2012, written into *Green Arrow* #0 after he had already appeared on *Arrow*.

TOMMY MERLYN

Tommy Merlyn was Oliver Queen's lifelong best friend. The son of billionaire industrialist Malcolm Merlyn, Tommy joined Oliver for many nights of debauchery in their wild adolescent days, partying and spending money as fast as their fathers could make it.

Tommy is one of the first to welcome Oliver back following his five-year stay on Lian Yu, and is disappointed to see that Oliver's hard-partying days are clearly over. And although he is glad his best friend is still alive, Tommy has a secret: he and Laurel Lance, Oliver's old flame, began a romantic relationship after Oliver was presumed dead.

In "Muse of Fire" (season 1, episode 7), Tommy was forced to grow up quickly, as his father cut him off financially. When he confronted his father about it, Malcolm claimed to have frozen the trust fund because Tommy couldn't use it reasonably, and that it was time for Tommy to get a job. Malcolm then went even further by seizing both Tommy's car and his apartment, leading Laurel to offer to let Tommy live with her for a while. Oliver offered Tommy a job at his club, Verdant.

Tommy's relationship with Oliver began to disintegrate in "Dead to Rights" (season 1, episode 16). When Deadshot attempted to assassinate Malcolm Merlyn, Oliver revealed himself as the Vigilante to Tommy in an effort to gain his trust and keep Malcolm alive.

Things between Tommy and Oliver took a turn for the worse in "Unfinished Business" (season 1, episode 19) after a girl died in Verdant from an overdose of Vertigo. The police, including Laurel's father, Detective Quentin Lance, believed they had evidence that pointed to Tommy giving the girl the Vertigo. Even though he was later cleared of all charges, Tommy was angry with Oliver for not trusting him or believing in his innocence. Tommy quit his job at Verdant, and informed Oliver that their friendship was over as well.

When Laurel's life was threatened following a contentious lawsuit in "Home Invasion" (season 1, episode 20), Tommy was forced to admit that the safest place for her was Queen Mansion, and asked Oliver if they could stay there until the threat was neutralized. Seeing Oliver and Laurel together reminded Tommy just how much the two still cared for each other, leading him to believe that Laurel would still choose Oliver if she were to find out he was the Vigilante. Once Oliver killed the assassin and Tommy and Laurel were safely back at home, he broke off the relationship, leaving without explaining why.

Oliver visited Tommy at his new office with the Merlyn Group in "Darkness on the Edge of Town" (season 1, episode 22) in an attempt to rebuild their relationship. He convinced Tommy that he had nothing to do with

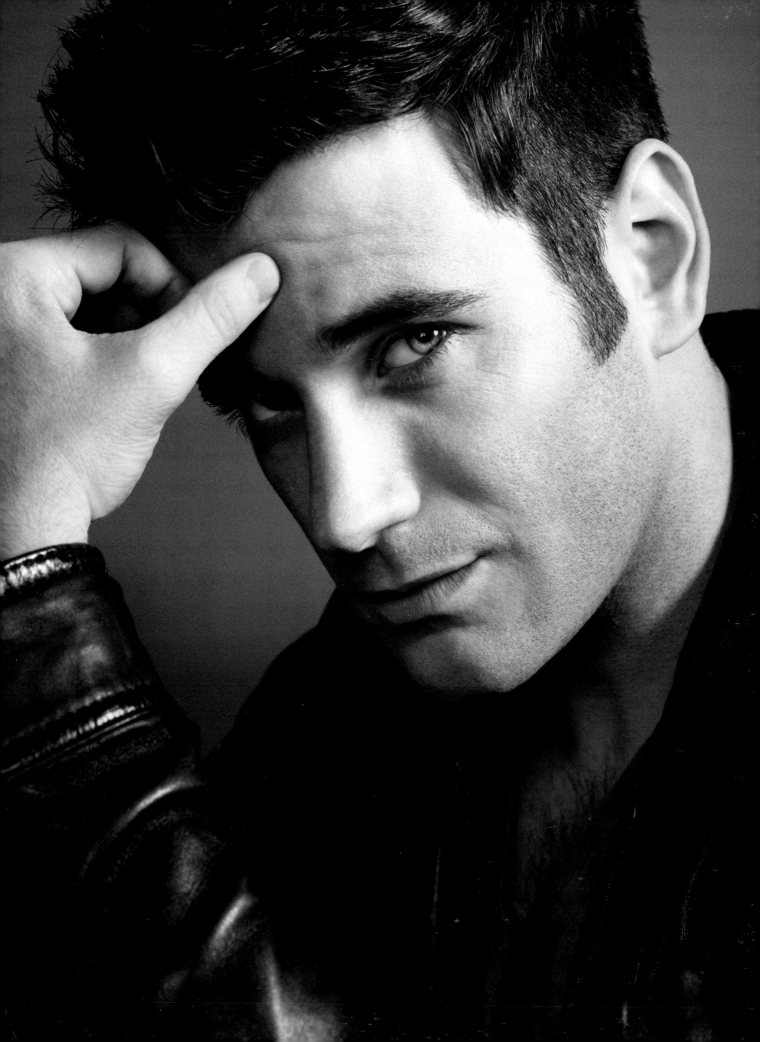

Tommy and Oliver were rivals for Laurel's affections for much of season 1, which caused some tension in their friendship.

Tommy's breakup with Laurel, and that Tommy should reconcile with her. But before Tommy could do that, Oliver realized that if he could stop Malcolm Merlyn and the Undertaking, his work as the Vigilante would be finished, and that he and Laurel could be together once more. So when Tommy visited Laurel to win her back, he was too late, and saw Oliver and Laurel kissing.

A drunken Tommy confronted Oliver about Laurel in "Sacrifice" (season 1, episode 23), but Oliver tried to tell him about his father's plan to destroy the Glades instead. Tommy refused to believe Oliver, later laughing about it to his father, only to be shocked when Malcolm freely admitted to his plan. Soon after Moira Queen's televized confession the police arrived to arrest Malcolm. Although he easily dispatched the officers, Tommy was knocked

unconscious in the struggle. When he awoke, Oliver and Diggle were there to take down his father, but Oliver made Tommy leave before he mortally wounded Malcolm.

Tommy made his way down to Laurel's office in the Glades as everything went to hell around them. Laurel was able to escape before the building collapsed, but Tommy was trapped inside, impaled by a length of steel rebar. Oliver made his way into the building, and was there as Tommy took his final breaths, becoming friends once again before Tommy died.

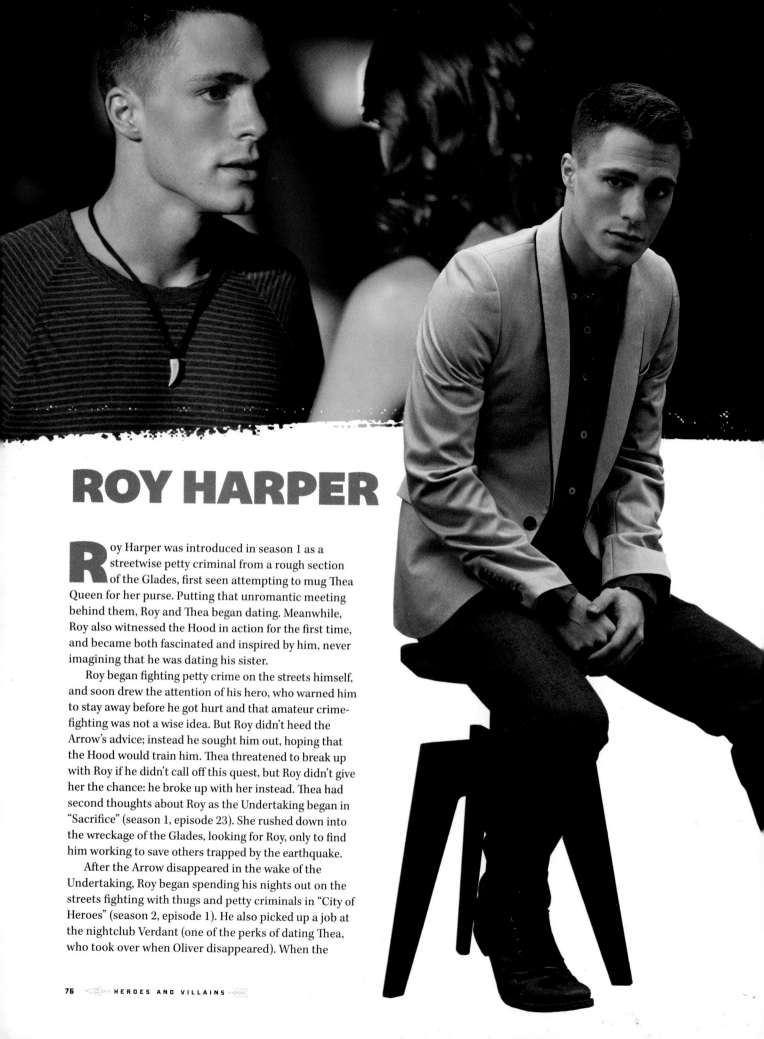

ROY HARPER

Roy Harper was introduced in season 1 as a streetwise petty criminal from a rough section of the Glades, first seen attempting to mug Thea Queen for her purse. Putting that unromantic meeting behind them, Roy and Thea began dating. Meanwhile, Roy also witnessed the Hood in action for the first time, and became both fascinated and inspired by him, never imagining that he was dating his sister.

Roy began fighting petty crime on the streets himself, and soon drew the attention of his hero, who warned him to stay away before he got hurt and that amateur crime-fighting was not a wise idea. But Roy didn't heed the Arrow's advice; instead he sought him out, hoping that the Hood would train him. Thea threatened to break up with Roy if he didn't call off this quest, but Roy didn't give her the chance: he broke up with her instead. Thea had second thoughts about Roy as the Undertaking began in "Sacrifice" (season 1, episode 23). She rushed down into the wreckage of the Glades, looking for Roy, only to find him working to save others trapped by the earthquake.

After the Arrow disappeared in the wake of the Undertaking, Roy began spending his nights out on the streets fighting with thugs and petty criminals in "City of Heroes" (season 2, episode 1). He also picked up a job at the nightclub Verdant (one of the perks of dating Thea, who took over when Oliver disappeared). When the

FACT SHEET

Portrayed by: Colton Haynes

Aliases: none

Current Status: alive

Relationships: Thea Queen (estranged girlfriend), Team Arrow

Comics History: Roy Harper was introduced as Green Arrow's sidekick Speedy way back in *More Fun Comics* #73. He got a new, more adult, persona in *The New Titans* #99, as he became known as Arsenal. In more recent years, Roy has fought crime as Red Arrow. He is a founding member of the Teen Titans.

Growing up in the rough-and-tumble Glades neighborhood, Roy has seen his fair share of hard knocks.

Arrow finally returned to Starling City, he was impressed with Roy's dedication to the cause, if not the danger he constantly put himself in, and asked Roy to be his eyes and ears in the Glades—partly because Oliver realized how important Roy was becoming to Thea.

While investigating the disappearance of a friend in "The Scientist" (season 1, episode 8), Roy stumbled into Sebastian Blood's plot to create a mirakuru-infused army. Roy showed Oliver a picture of his friend Max bleeding from his eyes, which Oliver instantly recognized as a mirakuru-related symptom thanks to his experience with the drug on Lian Yu. He warned Roy to stay away from it, but Roy, misunderstanding the Arrow's intentions, quit angrily, intent on solving Max's disappearance himself. The Arrow then shot Roy in the leg with an arrow to slow down his investigation and keep him and his friends—including Thea—safe.

But the wounded leg barely slowed Roy down, and he continued his investigation in "Three Ghosts" (season 2, episode 9), only to be captured by Cyrus Gold and brought to Brother Blood, who injected Roy with the mirakuru. This at first seemed like a good thing to Roy, because he felt better than ever after the Arrow rescued him. His Arrow-inflicted leg wound healed completely and he began to exhibit super-

strength and reflexes as well. The mirakuru serum also brought out a dark side in Roy, as the simmering anger just beneath the surface that had always been inside him frequently blossomed into an uncontrollable rage. After beating a criminal nearly to death in "Blind Spot" (season 2, episode 11), Roy was contacted by the Arrow with a promise to hone his new abilities and train him to control his anger.

In order to keep Roy from beating Bronze Tiger to death with his enhanced strength in "Tremors" (season 2, episode 12), the Arrow unmasked and revealed himself as Oliver Queen. He managed to convince Roy to use his feelings for Thea as a focal point for his newfound strength. The next morning, Oliver brought Roy to the Arrowcave and introduced him to Diggle and Felicity as the newest member of the team.

Roy continued to struggle with keeping his rage under control. Knowing the danger Roy presented to Théa, Oliver encouraged him to stay away from his sister for her own safety. Roy tried breaking up with Thea in "Birds of Prey" (season 2, episode 17), but she wouldn't accept it. Roy then resorted to making out with a random girl from the club, ensuring that Thea would see him and become angry enough to break up with him.

Roy was captured by Slade Wilson and Isabel Rochev in "The Man Under the Hood" (season 2, episode 19)

"FOR THE RECORD, DON'T CALL ME SPEEDY."

Roy is often shown wearing a red hoodie, a reference to his comic book alter egos Red Arrow and Arsenal.

and was strapped into a machine that allowed them to transfuse his mirakuru-laced blood into an army of ex-convicts that they planned to use to destroy Starling City. The Arrow rescued Roy from the contraption, but not before the deed had been done. Roy then went insane from the mirakuru and rampaged across town, going as far as killing a police officer in "Seeing Red" (season 2, episode 20). The Canary decided that the only way to truly stop Roy would be to kill him—unless they wanted to make the same mistake they made by not ending Slade Wilson's life years ago. But the Arrow was able to sedate Roy instead, bringing him back to the Arrowcave to keep him safe while the team figured out how to cure him.

When S.T.A.R. Labs developed a cure for the mirakuru, they delivered it to the Arrow for use on Slade's army, which was now engaged in a night of terror that looked

"IF YOU'LL EXCUSE ME, I NEED TO GET BACK TO MY LIFE OF CRIME."

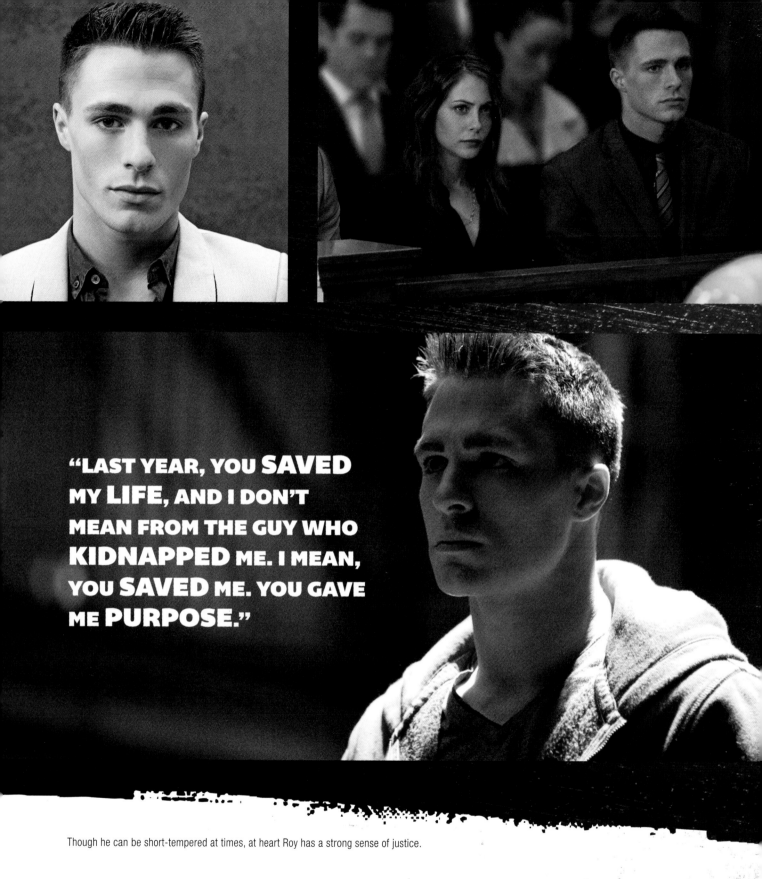

"LAST YEAR, YOU **SAVED** MY **LIFE**, AND I DON'T MEAN FROM THE GUY WHO **KIDNAPPED** ME. I MEAN, YOU **SAVED** ME. YOU GAVE ME **PURPOSE**."

Though he can be short-tempered at times, at heart Roy has a strong sense of justice.

like it would leave Starling City nothing more than a pile of smoking rubble. After a lot of deliberation, Oliver tested it first on Roy... and cured him. Roy then joined Oliver and his crew in battle against Slade's army. When the battle was over, and the heroes victorious, Roy returned home to find only a letter—Thea was gone, fed up with everyone lying to her, including him. She knew that he could not give up his red-hooded vigilante ways.

FACT SHEET

Portrayed by: Bex Taylor-Klaus

Aliases: Cindy (her given name)

Current Status: alive

Relationships: unnamed parents (deceased)

Comics History: In the comics, Sin is the foster daughter of Dinah Lance, the Black Canary. She is a martial arts expert once trained to be the next Lady Shiva.

Although she initially disliked him, Sin soon became good friends with Roy.

SIN

Sin is a young wayward street kid who has close relationships with Roy Harper and the Canary. Raised by a single father after her mother died of cancer when she was only a toddler, Sin was orphaned when her father's plane was shot down over Lian Yu. Her father died from his wounds suffered in the crash, but not before asking Sara Lance to find his daughter and look after her.

Sara did indeed get in touch with Sin when she returned to Starling City, which led to Sin meeting Roy Harper during his quest to find Sara's alter ego, the Canary. Sin led him to the Canary's hideaway in the clock tower, where she knocked him unconscious and left him to be questioned. The Canary convinced Sin that Roy was harmless, so she let him go, and the two grew to be friends. Through this friendship, Sin was introduced to Thea Queen. Sin was initially distrustful of Thea, believing her to be just another spoiled rich girl, but the two grew to be close friends.

After Roy's injection with the Mirakuru serum, Sin witnessed several instances of her friend losing control. In "Blind Spot" (season 2, episode 11) she posed as a prostitute to entice a judge with a penchant for murdering working girls. Roy saved the day, but in the process beat the man to within an inch of his life before Sin was able to calm him down.

In "Seeing Red" (season 2, episode 20) Sin came across Roy in a near-zombie state, now completely in the throes of the mirakuru. She tried to stop several of her friends from attacking Roy, but was too late as Roy attacked them instead, even knocking her down in the ensuing melee. Still, she stood by her friend, stopping the Canary from killing him.

> ## "I JUST LOVE WHEN PEOPLE COME BACK FROM THE DEAD. YOU KNOW, JUICES MY ZOMBIE FETISH."

BARRY ALLEN

Barry Allen is a member of the Central City police forensics team who journeyed to Starling City in "The Scientist" (season 2, episode 8) to investigate a superhuman thief who stole a centrifuge from Queen Consolidated. Barry's appearance was also designed as a prequel for The CW's newest Super Hero drama, *The Flash*.

Oliver quickly determined that Barry's visit was not quite as it seemed, and discovered that he had not come to Starling City in any official police capacity, but rather on his own personal time searching for superpowered beings, hopeful to find the one he believes to be responsible for the murder of his mother many years ago. Angry with Barry's deception, Oliver sent him packing back to Central City.

But while tracking the thief, Oliver was injected with a poison of unknown origin. At her wit's end, with no other alternatives for help with an antidote, Felicity called the smartest person she knew (and one she had romantic notions towards): Barry Allen. He was able to concoct a viable antidote that saved Oliver's life, and in doing so was entrusted with the Arrow's secret identity. Before leaving town, Barry gave Oliver an eye mask of his own design, one that allows the Arrow to conceal his true identity more easily than with the greasepaint mask he previously sported.

Barry returned to Central City, where he was hard at work in his own private lab on the night the S.T.A.R. Labs Particle Accelerator was finally tested. A giant electrical storm ensued, and Barry was doused in a chemical fire that left him alive, barely, but in a coma. What happens next is revealed in the spin-off series *The Flash*.

FACT SHEET

Portrayed by: Grant Gustin
Aliases: the Flash
Current Status: alive
Relationships: Henry Allen (father), Nora Allen (mother, deceased)

Comics History: As the Flash, Barry Allen is one of comics' most enduring Super Heroes. First appearing in 1956's *Showcase* #4, Barry was the second man to don the mantle of the Flash, following Jay Garrick.

FACT SHEET

Portrayed by: Adrian Holmes
Aliases: none
Current Status: alive
Relationships: unknown

Comics History: Frank Pike has yet to appear in the comics.

FRANK PIKE

Franklin Pike is a lieutenant with the SCPD, and Quentin Lance's superior officer. Early on during the Arrow's war on crime, Pike took a more pragmatic approach to the Vigilante than did Lance; while they agreed that the Arrow was dangerous and needed to be stopped, Pike did have an appreciation for the reduction in the crime rate the Arrow caused.

When Lance came to Pike in "Sacrifice" (season 1, episode 23) with information that Malcolm Merlyn was planning to destroy the Glades, Pike was hesitant to act until Lance revealed his source: the Arrow. Pike immediately suspended Lance for aiding and abetting the Vigilante. Not long after that, he demoted Lance from detective back to beat cop for his actions.

But the tactic failed, as Lance spent even more time in the following months working with the Arrow. When Slade Wilson's mirakuru army attacked Starling City at the end of season 2, Pike reinstated Lance to the rank of detective, putting him in charge of the counterattack against Slade's men; Pike reasoned that no one else on the police force knew as much about what they were dealing with than the officer who moonlighted with the Arrow.

FACT SHEET

Portrayed by: Janina Gavankar
Aliases: none
Current Status: alive
Relationships: unknown sister

Comics History: McKenna Hall has yet to appear in the comics, but she shares some commonalities with Melody McKenna, a Gotham City police detective with a grudge against Super Heroes.

McKENNA HALL

McKenna Hall was a detective with the Starling City Police Department who briefly dated Oliver Queen during the first season of *Arrow*. When the Hood needed help from the SCPD to take down the Count and stop the flow of the deadly drug Vertigo into the city, Oliver went to McKenna, an old friend from his wild partying days who had surprisingly joined the police force during Oliver's five-year absence.

One thing led to another, and soon the pair had rekindled their old romance. Meanwhile, Detective Quentin Lance recognized a kindred spirit in McKenna,

and appealed to her strong dislike for vigilantes in recruiting her to help him uncover the Hood's identity. McKenna and Lance stumbled upon the truth in "The Huntress Returns" (season 1, episode 17) as Helena Bertinelli (another love interest of Oliver's) told them point blank that Oliver Queen was the Hood, but neither cop believed her. Soon thereafter, McKenna was shot by Helena (as the Huntress) and left paralyzed. When Oliver visited her in the hospital, she revealed to him that she would be doing her rehab in Coast City, bringing a gentle end to their promising relationship.

"WHEN YOU **BELIEVE** IN WHAT YOU DO, YOU FIND A WAY TO MAKE IT **WORK**."

SLADE WILSON

Oliver's relationship with Slade went back a long way, to when he first arrived on Lian Yu.

Slade Wilson was an Australian Special Intelligence Service (ASIS) operative assigned in 2006 to a covert operation on the island of Lian Yu. He and his partner Billy Wintergreen were tasked with rescuing Yao Fei, a Chinese military commander banished to the island to help conceal a massacre orchestrated several years prior. At the same time, they were to uncover the scheme of one Edward Fyers, the mercenary holding Yao Fei hostage on the island for reasons unknown. But the two ASIS agents didn't even land on the island, as Fyers' men shot down their plane. Fyers gave them a chance to join his cause, whatever that might be, an offer that Wintergreen accepted and Slade declined, leaving him Fyers' prisoner. Yao Fei and Slade were eventually able to escape together, and planned to leave the island by stealing the supply plane that would soon be arriving on Fyers' airstrip.

Before they could enact their plot, they were separated, and each man encountered a recent arrival to the island, Oliver Queen, who had washed ashore as the only survivor of a shipwreck. After some initial misgivings, Slade began to train Oliver as a potential partner in his mission to escape the island. They were soon joined by a young woman they rescued named Shado, who was revealed to be Yao Fei's daughter, brought to the island by Fyers to use as leverage to ensure her father went along with his plans. Although Yao Fei was murdered and the supply plane destroyed, Slade, Oliver, and Shado were ultimately successful in ridding the island of Fyers and his men, with Oliver firing a fatal arrow into Fyers' chest.

In the ensuing months on the island, Slade and Shado continued to mentor and train Oliver in combat skills. Oliver and Shado grew romantically closer, something that eventually ate away at Slade, as he also had feelings for her. When another gang of mercenaries arrived on the island, the trio found themselves engaged in warfare once more. This new group was led by Dr. Anthony Ivo, who was searching the island for the fabled mirakuru, a World War II-era serum that was alleged to have given recipients super-strength, super-agility, and amazing healing powers. When Slade was severely wounded in a battle with Ivo's men, Oliver and Shado, along with Sara Lance (who they rescued from Ivo), joined the hunt for the mirakuru, figuring it was the only thing on the island that could possibly save Slade. After they found the serum aboard a Japanese submarine, Oliver injected it into Slade, then watched as he collapsed with no pulse, blood pouring from his eyes. The others believed him to be

Trained as a special forces soldier, and hardened by his struggle to survive on Lian Yu, Slade Wilson is a truly formidable opponent.

dead, but that wasn't the case; when he awoke, he saw Ivo shoot Shado in the head while Oliver and Sara watched. With his mirakuru-enhanced abilities, he slaughtered Ivo's entire squad, although the villainous doctor escaped into the jungle.

It soon became clear to Oliver and Sara that the mirakuru had affected Slade's mind, as he became prone to fits of the blackest rage imaginable. Invoking the names of both Shado and Slade's son Joe, Oliver was able to convince Slade to destroy the remaining mirakuru, lest it fall into the wrong hands.

They made a plan to attack Ivo's ship, the *Amazo*, and take care of the doctor once and for all, but once they reached the freighter, Slade overheard the truth of what had really happened to Shado: Ivo had given Oliver a choice of saving either Shado or Sara, and he chose

"THE ISLAND DIDN'T MAKE YOU **STRONG**, KID. IT REVEALED YOU TO BE WEAK."

Slade arrived in Starling City determined to get revenge on Oliver, blaming him for Shado's death.

Sara. Enraged, Slade attacked Oliver and imprisoned him alongside Ivo, taking over the freighter and promising that he would make Oliver suffer the same way he himself suffered before he kills him.

Spurred on by increasingly violent hallucinations of Shado, Slade took on Oliver in a final battle inside the burning, sinking *Amazo*. Oliver hit Slade with several arrows, but the mirakuru gave Slade the upper hand until rubble fell from the ceiling, trapping him beneath it. Oliver then had the choice to either kill Slade or inject him with the mirakuru cure, but believing that the cure might not stop Slade from continuing to seek his warped vengeance, Oliver stabbed Slade in the eye with an arrow, leaving him for dead aboard the stricken *Amazo* as it slowly sank to the bottom of the ocean.

But Slade did not die. Instead, he swam to the nearest coastline as the mirakuru regenerated all of his wounds except for his destroyed eye, eventually becoming a feared mercenary codenamed by A.R.G.U.S. as Deathstroke.

As news of Oliver Queen's survival and return to the world spread, Slade began plotting his ultimate, final revenge. He installed Isabel Rochev inside Queen Consolidated, and began funding the mayoral campaign of city council member Sebastian Blood. Slade also had Blood form a cult that would find people to test a new

strain of mirakuru, so that he could perfect the serum before unleashing an army of super-soldiers on Starling City and destroy the one thing that Oliver loved most.

Slade made his way to Starling City in the guise of a campaign supporter for Moira Queen's run for mayor, earning himself an invitation to the Queen Mansion, where Oliver reacted as if he'd seen a ghost (and in many ways, he had). Shortly afterwards, Slade gave Thea Queen a ride home in his limousine and told her about her true parentage—that she was actually the daughter of mass murderer Malcolm Merlyn—and then had her kidnapped by Brother Blood in an effort to force Moira Queen to drop out of the race.

Slade's plan picked up momentum at this point, as his plant Isabel Rochev forced Oliver out as Queen Consolidated CEO. He also hijacked a prison bus transferring prisoners, using the men aboard as the soldiers for his mirakuru army, and revealed to Laurel Lance that Oliver Queen was actually the Arrow.

Slade's next move was his most dastardly: he kidnapped the entire Queen family, then forced Oliver to choose which of the women in his life—his mother Moira or his sister Thea—he would save while the other died in a perverse reflection of Oliver's choice on the island between Sara and Shado. But Moira wouldn't let Oliver choose; instead, she stood and begged Slade to kill her

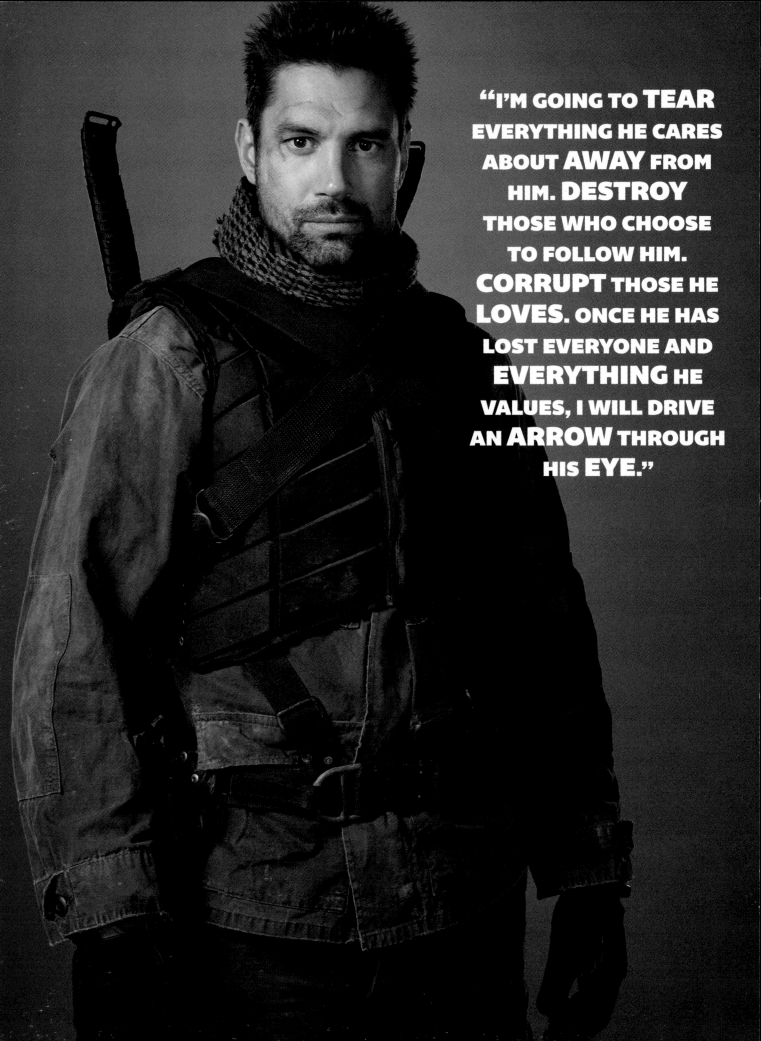

"I'M GOING TO **TEAR** EVERYTHING HE CARES ABOUT **AWAY** FROM HIM. **DESTROY** THOSE WHO CHOOSE TO FOLLOW HIM. **CORRUPT** THOSE HE **LOVES**. ONCE HE HAS LOST EVERYONE AND **EVERYTHING** HE VALUES, I WILL DRIVE AN **ARROW** THROUGH HIS **EYE**."

Lian Yu was the proving ground where both Slade and Oliver underwent traumatic transformational experiences. It made Oliver stronger, but for Slade the island served only to drive him to the point of madness.

instead of Thea, which he was more than happy to do, impaling her with his sword in front of her two children.

Slade turned his mirakuru army loose on the city soon thereafter. Then he made his final move, capturing both Felicity Smoak and Laurel Lance to force Oliver to choose between the two women he loved most in the world. While Oliver tried to talk Slade out of killing either one of them, Felicity injected a hidden syringe filled with the mirakuru cure into Slade's neck, eliminating his superhuman powers. In the battle that ensued, Oliver

once again gained the upper hand, and was left with the choice whether or not to kill Slade. Oliver knocked him unconscious and delivered him to a prison back on Lian Yu, the same place they had met so many years before.

Greg Berlanti summarizes their relationship: "Slade was mentor, friend, and brother to Oliver. It was a devastating blow to him to watch his friend be perverted by the mirakuru. He put a lot of faith in Slade as they worked to get off the island, and to lose a friend in such a way was hard to walk away from."

YAO FEI

"YOUR **TIME** ON THIS **ISLAND** IS AT AN **END.**"

The first person Oliver Queen encountered during his five years on the island, Yao Fei had come to Lian Yu in exile. A former general in the People's Liberation Army, he had been forced by his superiors to take the fall for a highly controversial military massacre. Following his public shaming, Yao Fei was sent to Lian Yu and was captured soon thereafter by Edward Fyers. Fyers was a mercenary on a mission to destabilize the Chinese economy by shooting down Ferris Air flights crossing the island into China.

Yao Fei was joined in captivity by Australian special agent Slade Wilson, and the pair teamed up to escape Fyers' cell. Yao Fei then ran across Oliver Queen, who had recently washed ashore following a shipwreck. He took Oliver under his wing, teaching him basic survival skills, like hunting with a bow and arrow (which comes in very handy later on). He also tried to teach Oliver how to forget, telling him that he would never survive their ordeal if all he did was stare at Laurel's photograph.

When Oliver was captured by Fyers' soldiers, Yao Fei went to free Oliver, not wanting his own camp's location revealed. He left Oliver with medicinal herbs to nurse himself back to health following his torture at the hands of Fyers' men, but then Yao Fei was recaptured by Fyers, and this time it was Oliver who came to his rescue. Unexpectedly, Yao Fei turned on him during this attempt, and, in a bewildering turn of events, it appeared that he had been working alongside Fyers the entire time.

Yao Fei took Oliver to a fighting pit, where he beat the younger man senseless and appeared to kill him. But before dumping Oliver's body into a river, ostensibly to dispose of it, Yao Fei stuffed a map into Oliver's pocket. Yao Fei then learned that Fyers had brought his daughter Shado to the island, keeping her captive in order to ensure Yao Fei's loyalty. As a reward for "killing" Oliver, Yao Fei was given five minutes alone with Shado.

After a firefight with Oliver and Slade on one side and Fyers' men (including Yao Fei) on the other, Oliver, Slade, and Shado (having now escaped and joined their group) were captured once more. Fyers threatened to kill all three of them unless Yao Fei recorded a video claiming responsibility for shooting down the Ferris Air flights. Revealing that his true loyalty was to his daughter and friends all along, Yao Fei made the video, but by doing so he used up all of his value to Fyers, who promptly shot him in the head.

Yao Fei's clothing and skill with a bow inspire Oliver to adopt the same guise when he returns to Starling City and becomes the Hood.

FACT SHEET

Portrayed by: Byron Mann
Aliases: none
Current Status: deceased
Relationships: Shado (daughter, deceased), Oliver Queen (protégé)

Comics History: In the comics, Yao Fei is Accomplished Perfect Physician, a member of China's Super Hero team The Great Ten.

FACT SHEET

Portrayed by: Celina Jade
Aliases: none
Current Status: deceased
Relationships: Yao Fei (father, deceased), Oliver Queen (lover)

Comics History: Shado is an orphan raised by the Yakuza to be the ultimate killing machine. She was first an enemy, then an ally, of Green Arrow.

SHADO

Shado was the daughter of Yao Fei. After her father, a former general in the People's Liberation Army, went missing, Shado spent years looking for him. One night, several men came to her home claiming to have information about her father's location; but the men were actually Fyers' soldiers, who abducted her and brought her to the island. This was to make sure that Yao Fei played his role in Fyers' scheme to destabilize the Chinese economy.

Shado was able to free herself in "Salvation" (season 1, episode 18), using a firefight between Slade and Oliver and Fyers' men as cover to take down several of her captors. She escaped into the jungle with Oliver and Slade, and before long was training Oliver in the use of Yao Fei's bow and arrow. Shado also shared a kiss with Oliver, but both of them stopped before it went any further.

Shado, Oliver, and Slade were once again captured by Fyers in "Darkness on the Edge of Town" (season 1, episode 22), and were used as leverage to get Yao Fei to record a false confessional video claiming responsibility for shooting down the Ferris Air jets over Lian Yu. Yao Fei recorded the video begrudgingly, and was then shot in the head and killed by Fyers. In the confusion that followed, Oliver freed himself with a knife slipped to him by Yao Fei, then freed Shado and Slade. Oliver and Shado managed to redirect the missile, keeping it from hitting the plane, and instead destroying Fyers' camp. In the aftermath of all the destruction, Fyers took Shado hostage, intending to use her as a bargaining chip for his own freedom. But Oliver fired an arrow, striking Fyers in the chest and killing him.

The next five months were peaceful on the island; Oliver continued to train with Shado, who took to wearing her father's hood as a way to honor him. Their relationship grew intimate as well. But this peace was shattered by the arrival of another group of mercenaries, one of whom Oliver beat to death with a rock, leaving him distraught with guilt.

Using a map taken from the dead man, Oliver, Shado, and Slade found a small cave containing the bodies of several WWII-era Japanese soldiers. But then the old supply plane they were using as a camp was fired upon by a ship anchored offshore, and Slade ended up with several nasty burns on his face from the explosions. Both the mercenaries and the ship were commanded by Dr. Anthony Ivo, who had come to Lian Yu in search of the legendary mirakuru serum. Oliver and Shado made plans to get the serum from Ivo in order to heal Slade, who was suffering badly from the wounds he had sustained.

Dr. Ivo brought more than trouble to Lian Yu; he also brought Sara Lance, whom Oliver thought had been lost at sea following the wreck of the *Queen's Gambit*. Shado was disturbed to learn the unfaithful nature of Oliver's character before the accident, leaving her own relationship with Oliver in question. Oliver, Shado, and Sara found the mirakuru in the wreckage of an old Japanese submarine, and just before they injected Slade, he confessed his own romantic feelings for Shado. The mirakuru caused Slade to scream in pain as blood poured out of his eyes and his pulse stopped.

Oliver and Shado had no time to mourn the apparent death of their friend, as Ivo's men found them and took them captive. But there would be no escape for Shado this time; she was shot in the head and killed by Ivo. Shado was buried next to Yao Fei and Robert Queen.

EDWARD FYERS

Edward Fyers was a mercenary encountered by Oliver Queen in the early days of his five years on the island of Lian Yu. Fyers was hired by an undisclosed employer to set up camp on a deserted Pacific island and shoot down Ferris Air flights heading into and out of China, in an attempt to destabilize the Chinese economy. Fyers, in true mercenary fashion, did not care who his employer was, but it was later revealed to be Amanda Waller, head of A.R.G.U.S.

At some point early in their stay on Lian Yu, Fyers' men found a castaway lurking on the edge of their camp: Oliver Queen. Fyers showed him a picture of Yao Fei in "Damaged" (season 1, episode 5), but Oliver pretended not to know him in order to keep his friend safe. Fyers wasn't buying it, and brought in soldier Billy Wintergreen to torture Oliver. Oliver refused to crack, though, and Fyers ordered Wintergreen to kill him; but before he could do so, Fyers' men were attacked by a man in a hood with a bow and arrows—Yao Fei.

Fyers needed Yao Fei for the final piece of his plan, a video that Yao Fei would record taking responsibility for bringing down the Ferris Air flights. In order to force Yao Fei into doing this, Fyers kidnapped his daughter Shado to use as leverage. Yao Fei acquiesced and recorded the video—just before Fyers shot him in the head, killing him.

But Fyers' plan fell apart for good in "Sacrifice" (season 1, episode 23), as Oliver redirected the missile intended for the airliner, sending it instead into Fyers' camp, destroying nearly everything there. Fyers then took Shado hostage, furious with the young interloper who had wrecked his plans. Showing that he had changed since arriving on the island, Oliver shot Fyers using Yao Fei's bow, killing him on the spot.

FACT SHEET

Portrayed by: Sebastian Dunn

Aliases: none

Current Status: deceased

Relationships: none

Comics History: Edward Fyers was a mercenary in the comics as well, working as a contractor for the CIA. He and Green Arrow were close allies, working together on many occasions.

Pragmatic and ruthless, Edward Fyers will do anything to fulfill his mission, including the torture and execution of prisoners.

BILLY WINTERGREEN

FACT SHEET

Portrayed by: Jeffrey Robinson
Aliases: none
Current Status: deceased
Relationships: Slade Wilson (former best friend)

Comics History: William Wintergreen served in the British Army in the comics, where he met Slade Wilson, and was best man at his wedding. As Slade morphed into Deathstroke the Terminator, Wintergreen served as his right-hand man and moral conscience.

Billy Wintergreen arrived on the island as a member of Slade Wilson's Australian Special Intelligence Service team, which was sent there to free Yao Fei from captivity. To save his own neck, Wintergreen turned on Wilson and joined Fyers' men, where he tortured Oliver Queen.

After his escape, Oliver partnered with Slade for an assault on a supply aircraft, which they intended to use to leave the island. Slade revealed to Oliver plans for an airstrike to take out Fyers' operation; Oliver then went back into Fyers' camp to rescue Yao Fei and spare him from the airstrike, only to be recaptured himself. Slade then arrived at the camp, having followed Oliver, and rescued him, killing his old partner Billy Wintergreen in the process.

"COME **BACK**
TO **DIE?"**

A former friend of Slade Wilson, Billy throws in his lot with Edward Fyers and becomes his right-hand man, ever willing to do his dirty work.

FACT SHEET

Portrayed by: Dylan Neal
Aliases: none
Current Status: deceased
Relationships: Jessica Ivo (wife)

Comics History: Professor Anthony Ivo is one of the premier mad-scientist inventors of the comics. In his first appearance, he menaced the Justice League with his android creation (and "son"), Amazo.

DR. ANTHONY IVO

Cut from the same mad-scientist cloth as so many before him, Dr. Anthony Ivo sought to unearth a legendary Japanese serum from the days of World War II: mirakuru, which gave its subjects superhuman powers and abilities. His search for the sunken submarine believed to house mirakuru led Ivo to the island of Lian Yu. He arrived in his prison freighter *Amazo*, full of test subjects upon which he was experimenting.

Following the shipwreck of the *Queen's Gambit*, Sara Lance awoke to find herself in a cell aboard the *Amazo* as Ivo's latest prisoner. Ivo took an instant liking to her and released the young woman, taking her back to his quarters where he explained to her that he was a scientist who intended to "save the human race."

Ivo took Sara under his wing, and used some good old-fashioned Stockholm syndrome to assist him in any manner of unspeakable experiments. Sometime later, Ivo captured another *Queen's Gambit* survivor, as Oliver Queen ended up aboard the *Amazo*. Ivo and his men took Oliver and Sara back to Lian Yu, intending to have Oliver lead them to the grave full of Japanese soldiers located on the island. But Shado and Slade Wilson saved him and Sara, and the foursome escaped into the jungle.

Slade was injected with the mirakuru serum in "The Scientist" (season 2, episode 8), which stopped his heart. Ivo then took Oliver, Sara, and Shado captive once more, and decided to play a cruel game with Oliver. In a moment that echoes throughout the rest of the second season, Ivo forced Oliver to decide which of the two women he should kill. When the madman looked to be about to shoot Sara, Oliver leaped toward Ivo in an attempt to stop him, but could only watch as Ivo shot and killed Shado, just as Slade Wilson reappeared. Fueled by the mirakuru serum, Slade killed most of Ivo's men, forcing the evil doctor to flee back to the *Amazo*.

In "The Promise" (season 2, episode 15) Oliver allowed himself to be captured once more, as part of his plan to take the freighter and free all his former fellow prisoners. As he and Slade went after Ivo, the doctor told Slade that Oliver chose Sara over Shado, and that he was the reason Slade's beloved Shado was dead. Enraged, Slade cut off Ivo's hand and turned on Oliver.

Ivo was slowly dying of gangrene after the loss of his hand, and knew it. In "The Man Under the Hood" (season 2, episode 19) he told Oliver and Sara that he had created a cure that counteracts the mirakuru serum. Ivo was willing to give them the location of this cure to help them stop Slade, but on one condition: they deliver him a quick death. They readily agreed to his deal, and Sara was prepared to shoot him. But Oliver stepped in and killed Ivo himself with a double shot to the chest, as he didn't want Sara to ever have to experience taking a life.

"IT'S **HARDER** THAN IT LOOKS, **ISN'T IT?** KILLING AN **UNARMED MAN.**"

THOMAS FLYNN

Reverend Thomas Flynn was a missionary working in Maliku, a small island in the Indian Ocean, when the *Amazo* docked there for supplies. Dr. Anthony Ivo asked Flynn to come aboard and administer last rites for a dying crewmember, but it was all a ruse; once Flynn boarded, he was imprisoned and spent over a year in a jail cell aboard the ship.

Flynn told this story to Oliver Queen when Oliver was captured by Ivo, and introduced Oliver to his pet rat Abraham. During the freighter riot, Flynn escaped his cell alongside the other prisoners. When Hendrick Von Arnim attempted to choke Sara Lance to death, Flynn smashed him in the head with a pole and then ran, jumping off the boat and swimming to Lian Yu.

FACT SHEET

Portrayed by: James Pizzinato
Aliases: none
Current Status: unknown
Relationships: unknown

Comics History: Thomas Flynn has yet to appear in the comics.

HENRICK VON ARNIM

Hendrick Von Arnim was one of the prisoners aboard the *Amazo*. He disliked Oliver because of his friendship with Sara; he hated Sara due to her involvement with Ivo. When Oliver and Sara returned to set the prisoners free in "The Promise" (season 2, episode 15), Arnim tried to kill Sara, before being stopped by Thomas Flynn.

The prisoners made their way to the supply plane back on the island, but Slade requested that they send Arnim back to the ship to fix the engines. Anatoly Knyazev disarmed a mine and Sara used the explosives to turn Arnim into a human bomb, planning to detonate it once Arnim was close to Slade. He lived to fight another day, but Von Arnim did not.

FACT SHEET

Portrayed by: Artine Brown
Aliases: none
Current Status: deceased
Relationships: unknown

Comics History: Hendrick Von Arnim has yet to appear in the comics.

FACT SHEET

Portrayed by: Ronald Selmour

Aliases: the Butcher (real name unknown)

Current Status: deceased

Relationships: Dr. Anthony Ivo (employer)

Comics History: The Butcher has yet to appear in the comics.

THE BUTCHER

The Butcher was a crewmember of the *Amazo*. and a brutal sociopath. When the ship's captain failed to capture Slade Wilson and Shado, Ivo shot him in the head and promoted the Butcher.

When Oliver lit a fire on Lian Yu in "The Promise" (season 2, episode 15), Ivo sent the Butcher to recapture the escapee. They suspected it was a ploy of some sort, and gave Oliver truth serum, but Sara had injected Oliver with picrotoxin, which counteracted the sodium pentothal. Oliver tricked Ivo into sending his men into an ambush set up by Sara and Slade, and then he freed the prisoners.

After the crew took back control of the situation, the Butcher shot Slade, but the bullet barely slowed the mirakuru-enhanced soldier. Slade wrapped his hands around the Butcher's head and crushed his skull.

FACT SHEET

Portrayed by: John Barrowman
Aliases: The Dark Archer
Current Status: alive
Relationships: Rebecca Merlyn (wife, deceased), Tommy Merlyn (son, deceased), Thea Queen (daughter)

Comic History: Merlyn is a long-time *Green Arrow* villain. His skill with a bow rivals Green Arrow, and he is one of the world's foremost contract killers. He has also held membership in several criminal groups, including (but certainly not limited to) the Anti-Justice League, the Injustice League, the Killer Elite, the League of Assassins, and the Secret Society of Super-Villains. Merlyn is just an alias in the comics, however; his given name is Arthur King.

MALCOLM MERLYN

Malcolm Merlyn was a billionaire industrialist and one of the brightest lights in the Starling City business hierarchy. The best friend of fellow power broker Robert Queen, Malcolm was widowed years ago when his wife Rebecca was murdered in the crime-ridden Glades neighborhood of Starling City. Her death left Malcolm alone with his young son, Tommy; emotionally adrift, he began an affair with Robert Queen's wife Moira. This affair ultimately led to the birth of Moira's daughter, Thea, although both Malcolm and Robert were initially unaware of Thea's true parentage.

The affair only made things worse for Malcolm. Feeling guilty for betraying Rebecca's memory, he fled Starling City, eventually coming to rest in Nanda Parbat. There, he met a man known as Rā's al Ghūl, the mysterious leader of the deadly League of Assassins. Malcolm trained in their ways, then served with the League for two years before being released from his obligations by Rā's.

Upon his return to Starling City, Malcolm gathered a group of influential friends, Robert Queen and Frank Chen chief among them, and began developing a plan to rid the Glades of crime and rebuild it using the wealth of the criminals who had long profited from it. But when Malcolm revealed the final stage of his plan—namely, using an earthquake machine developed by Dr. Markov to level the Glades—several members of the group, including Robert Queen, felt he was taking it too far. Undeterred, Malcolm had Frank Chen rig Robert's yacht, the *Queen's Gambit*, with explosives, causing it to sink in the South Pacific, apparently killing everyone aboard, including Robert, his son Oliver, and Sara Lance.

With Robert and his conscience out of the way, Malcolm escalated his plan quickly. He forced Moira Queen to approve any and all scientific developments he needed through Queen Consolidated, threatening both her and Thea's life to get what he required.

Oliver Queen's surprising return from presumed death some five years later rattled Malcolm, and he pressured Moira into digging deep to find out just how much Oliver knew about the Undertaking project and his own father's involvement in it. Malcolm was also troubled by the simultaneous arrival of Starling City's new vigilante, the Hood, who seemed to be targeting all the names on the list of power brokers created by Malcolm, Robert, and Frank Chen all those years ago.

Based on the suspicious timing, Malcolm began to believe that Oliver could actually be the Hood, and sent a man to kill him; the assassin failed when he himself was killed by Detective Quentin Lance.

In "Year's End" (season 1, episode 9) Malcolm grew so frustrated with the Hood's interference in his business that he took up a persona of his own, the Dark Archer.

"ACCIDENTS TEND TO BEFALL PEOPLE WHO ARE TOO CURIOUS."

"YOU THINK **YOU** CAN **STOP** ME? EVEN THE **VIGILANTE** COULDN'T KILL ME."

Moira increasingly came to regret her involvement with Malcolm and the Undertaking, but found it difficult to extract herself from his schemes.

In this guise, he killed Adam Hunt with an arrow in an attempt to lure the Hood out of the shadows. He then killed Nelson Ravich in another failed attempt to trap the Hood, finally taking hostages in a factory. The Dark Archer and the Hood battled it out, with Malcolm nearly killing Oliver, but he managed to get away.

Malcolm was the subject of an assassination attempt himself in "Dead to Rights" (season 1, episode 16), as the Chinese Triad hired Deadshot to kill him at the behest of Moira Queen. Deadshot managed to hit Malcolm with a curare-laced bullet, but before Malcolm could die, the Hood arrived and convinced Tommy Merlyn to give his father a blood transfusion to rid his body of the poisoned blood. Moira visited Malcolm in the hospital afterwards, and he tasked her with finding out just who it was that had tried to have him killed.

Desperate to steer blame elsewhere, Moira pinned the attempted hit on Frank Chen, doctoring up evidence that would support her lie. The Dark Archer killed Chen and was about to kill Chen's young daughter as well, but was talked out of it by Moira, who was unaware of the Dark Archer's true identity.

In "Darkness on the Edge of Town" (season 1, episode 22), Malcolm began to tie up loose ends in preparation for the Undertaking. In the guise of the Dark Archer, he visited Unidac Industries and killed Dr. Markov and his team of scientists who had developed the earthquake machine. After admitting responsibility for the Unidac massacre to Moira Queen, Malcolm was visited by the Hood, who fired an arrow at him. Malcolm caught it in mid-air, revealing himself to be the Dark Archer. The two men engaged in hand-to-hand combat, from which Malcolm emerged victorious. He lifted the hood from his adversary's face, revealing him to be none other than Oliver Queen.

Malcolm imprisoned Oliver, then explained his motives before leaving to await the destruction of the Glades. Soon thereafter, Tommy came to visit Malcolm and told him that for some reason Oliver believed he wanted to destroy the Glades. This Malcolm freely admitted to, and he and Tommy watched on television as Moira Queen admitted both her and Malcolm's role in the Undertaking. The police arrived moments later, and Malcolm fled after killing all three of them.

But Malcolm's escape was short-lived, as the Hood and John Diggle soon caught up with him. The Hood and the Dark Archer engaged in one final round of battle, this one ending when the Hood stabbed Malcolm through the chest with one of his own arrows. The Hood and his allies had disabled the earthquake device, and Malcolm was grievously injured; all appeared well until Malcolm revealed that he had a second device hidden away somewhere else in the Glades,

"THIS **CITY** NEEDS WHAT IS ABOUT TO **HAPPEN** IN ORDER TO **SURVIVE**. THE PEOPLE WHO ARE **DESTROYING** IT FROM THE INSIDE NEED TO BE **ERASED** FROM THE MAP."

As the Dark Archer, Malcolm is a formidable foe, easily a match for Oliver Queen.

which then detonated. As the city crumbled around them, Malcolm fell to the ground, for all appearances dead.

However, Malcolm survived, though he kept it a secret for several months before revealing himself to Moira, claiming that it was he who had made sure the jury acquitted her in the Undertaking-related murder trial. He also triumphantly divulged that he had discovered Thea was actually his daughter.

Slade Wilson ended up being the one to break the unhappy news to Thea in "Deathstroke" (season 2, episode 18), a move that brought Malcolm back to Starling City as the Dark Archer, arriving just as Slade's army began to overrun the city. He saved Thea from one of Slade's rampaging goons, and then begged her to come with him to safety. But Thea didn't want anything to do with him, shooting Malcolm twice in the chest.

Malcolm survived certain death once more, thanks to a Kevlar vest. He told Thea that she was just like him—ready and willing to kill someone if that's what it took—and that he would be there when she needed him most. After finding out that Roy Harper was one of the Arrow's sidekicks, Thea ran back to Malcolm, and together they left Starling City.

Greg Berlanti has this to say on Malcolm's role in the Undertaking: "The Undertaking was the handiwork of Malcolm Merlyn, our big bad of season 1. He had a myopic view of right and wrong driven by the grief of the murder of his wife. He chose to wipe the 'cancer' of the Glades from Starling City. His machinations really set us up for a very exciting and emotional ride, with losses on all sides."

"YOUR MOTHER BUILT HER CLINIC IN THE GLADES BECAUSE SHE WANTED TO SAVE THIS CITY. IT CAN'T BE SAVED."

Malcolm learned how to fight during his time with the League of Assassins, becoming skilled at archery and hand-to-hand combat. His costume intentionally resembles that of the Arrow in an attempt to frame Oliver Queen for the murders he carries out.

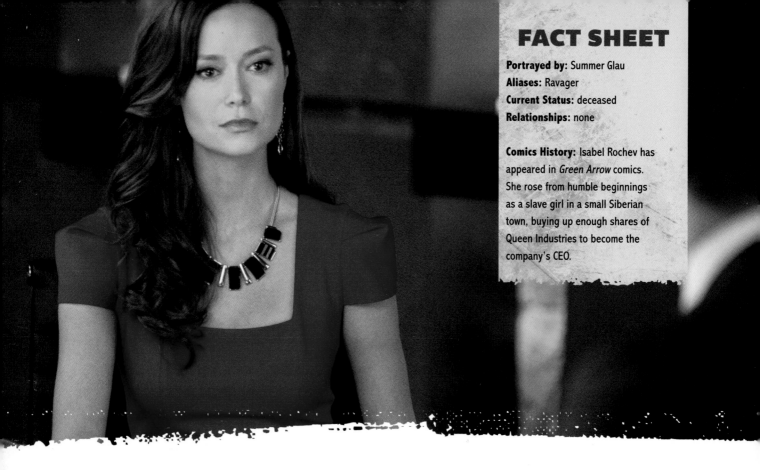

FACT SHEET

Portrayed by: Summer Glau
Aliases: Ravager
Current Status: deceased
Relationships: none

Comics History: Isabel Rochev has appeared in *Green Arrow* comics. She rose from humble beginnings as a slave girl in a small Siberian town, buying up enough shares of Queen Industries to become the company's CEO.

ISABEL ROCHEV

Isabel Rochev could have been a uniquely American success story: born in Moscow, she was adopted by an American family at the age of nine. She excelled academically, eventually finding her way into business school and a prestigious internship with Queen Consolidated. There, she caught the wandering eye of CEO Robert Queen, and the two began an affair. This relationship became more than just another dalliance for Robert, and he and Isabel began planning to run away together. But on the night of their intended departure, Robert's daughter Thea was injured in a horse-riding accident, and Robert rushed to her side. After that, instead of leaving with Isabel the next day, Robert came to his senses and fired her, never speaking to her again.

Isabel returned to Starling City several years later as a corporate raider intent on a hostile takeover of Queen Consolidated. In the second season premiere, "City of Heroes" (season 2, episode 1), Isabel was able to buy 45 percent of the company's shares, and was very close to the additional 10 percent she needed to effectively gain control of the company. But Oliver Queen came back in time to buy up an additional 5 percent himself, leaving him and Isabel as equal partners in the company.

In "Keep Your Enemies Closer" (season 2, episode 6) Isabel accompanied Oliver and his team on a business trip to Moscow. She shared her adoption story with Oliver over

drinks in the hotel bar, and the pair ended up sleeping together that night in Oliver's suite.

When Thea was kidnapped by Brother Blood in "Deathstroke" (season 2, episode 18), Oliver temporarily appointed Isabel as CEO of Queen Consolidated, which was akin to temporary insanity on his part. (Perhaps if he'd still been using his father's book, he would have noticed Isabel's name on the List and been forewarned never to trust her.) Not surprisingly, Isabel immediately called for an emergency board meeting and convinced them to make her appointment permanent. Isabel also revealed to Oliver that she had been working with his mortal enemy Slade Wilson the entire time, and only bought her initial shares as part of Slade's plan to draw Oliver back to Starling City.

In "The Man Under the Hood" (season 2, episode 19) Isabel revealed her relationship with Robert Queen to Oliver before trying to shoot him, only to be shot twice in the chest by Diggle and left for dead. However, one mirakuru injection later, Isabel was back among the living and looking for revenge once more.

In "City of Blood" (season 2, episode 22) Isabel made a dramatic return at Moira Queen's funeral, casually informing Diggle and Felicity that they'd be the next to die. As Slade's mirakuru army assaulted the city, Isabel suited up in a costume similar to Deathstroke's and

"IS THAT *BLOOD* ON YOUR **FACE**?"

In "City of Heroes" (season 2, episode 1) Isabel attempted a hostile takeover of Queen Consolidated, but ended up owning only half the shares, making her and Oliver equal partners. Their business relationship was best described as "strained."

attacked Diggle, who was attempting to plant bombs on a bridge to crush Slade's army. She proved to be too much for Diggle, and was about to finish him off when Felicity came charging in with a van and ran her over. But the mirakuru gave Isabel remarkable strength and stamina, and she lived to fight another day.

Well, a few more hours, anyway. She next went to Sebastian Blood's office and delivered a double-sword execution in retaliation for Blood giving the mirakuru cure to Oliver. But in her final battle in the Queen Consolidated boardroom, Isabel's neck was snapped by Nyssa al Ghūl, killing her once and for all.

"**IF** OLIVER'S **SMART,** HE **RAN BACK** TO HIS **ISLAND** TO **HIDE.**"

During Slade's attack on Starling City, Isabel dressed up in her own costume and became the Ravager.

FACT SHEET

Portrayed by: Kevin Alejandro
Aliases: Brother Blood
Current Status: deceased
Relationships: Maya Resik (mother, deceased), Sebastian Sangre (father, deceased)

Comics History: Sebastian Blood was the eighth man to hold the mantle of Brother Blood in the comics, battling the Teen Titans for the demon Trigon.

SEBASTIAN BLOOD

A native of the Glades, Sebastian Blood suffered tragedy as a young child after he killed his abusive, alcoholic father, with his mother taking the blame for it and ending up in a mental institution. This background made for good political capital as Blood grew up to become a city councilman, representing the same Glades neighborhood he grew up in.

Blood used the citywide groundswell of support for the Glades in the aftermath of the Undertaking to launch his campaign for mayor of Starling City. He immediately marked Oliver Queen and his family as a target for his campaign: symbols of the very corruption he railed against, the types of people that allowed it to happen in the first place. When Oliver no-showed at a fundraiser he and Blood had co-sponsored in "Identity" (season 2, episode 2), all of Blood's prejudices were confirmed.

Oliver attempted to make it up to Blood by setting up another fundraiser in "Crucible" (season 2, episode 4). This time it was a "cash for guns"-type event in the Glades, designed to both raise money and reduce the rising tide of gang activity in the neighborhood. But the event was attacked by a new crime boss, Xavier Reed, who called himself "the Mayor." After Xavier was stopped by the Arrow and arrested, Officer Daily brought him to see Blood. Sebastian wore a horrifying mask for this meeting, and the other men in the room called him

Brother Blood. He injected the Mayor with a serum he called mirakuru, with devastating effects—blood poured from Xavier's eyes, then he died.

Brother Blood recognized the obstacle that the Arrow would cause him when he finally went public with his plan, so he went after the Vigilante via back-door channels in "State v. Queen" (season 2, episode 7) by providing the Count with a new method for distributing his Vertigo drug. This did succeed in bringing out the Arrow, but the Count was killed instead of Oliver Queen.

Brother Blood finally found success with the mirakuru serum when he injected one of his most devout followers, Cyrus Gold. Not only did Gold survive the serum, but he turned into a superhuman instrument of Blood's will. Sebastian ordered Gold to break into a Queen Consolidated lab and steal a centrifuge, then rob a blood bank for some universal donor blood so he could manufacture more mirakuru.

Brother Blood was the face of the Blood Cult, but he was not the true mastermind. Slade Wilson was revealed to be the power behind the group in "Three Ghosts" (season 2, episode 9), as a part of his elaborate scheme to destroy Starling City.

Blood visited his mother in her psychiatric facility in "Blind Spot" (season 2, episode 11), killing her after discovering that she had told a snooping Laurel Lance

"**BLOOD** PROVIDES LIFE. BLOOD PROVIDES **POWER**. AND WITH **POWER**, THERE IS **NO LIMIT** TO WHAT **I CAN DO**."

After the Undertaking, Sebastian ran for mayor of Starling City, with Slade Wilson's backing.

the truth about his father's death. Sebastian was then warned by Slade Wilson to deal with Laurel, as her investigation was becoming a problem for the Blood Cult, so he had one of his disciples pose as Brother Blood and kidnap Laurel, thereby throwing suspicion off himself.

Moira Queen became a late entry into the field of candidates for mayor, as the Cult's business and personal agendas began to intersect. In "Deathstroke" (season 2, episode 18), Slade kidnapped Thea Queen and broadcast a video of the frightened girl in the middle of a mayoral debate between Sebastian Blood and Moira Queen. Blood was angry with Slade over this tactic, believing that the video would result in a massive sympathy vote for Moira and would hand her the election.

But Moira Queen didn't make it to election day. Following her murder at the hands of Slade, Blood was elected mayor of Starling City in "City of Blood" (season 2, episode 21). During his first days in office, Laurel Lance was able to bug his computer and, working with the

police department, determine that he had known about Moira's impending murder before it happened. But before Oliver could do anything with this information, Blood and Slade unleashed their army of mirakuru-enhanced soldiers on the city.

In "Streets of Fire" (season 2, episode 22), Blood realized that Slade was going to go much further than he had ever realized. Slade didn't intend to break and then rebuild Starling City into a better place; he planned to leave it a pile of smoking rubble. To that end, he stole the mirakuru cure and gave it to Oliver, as he was now aware of the Arrow's true identity. He told Oliver that the mask he wore was the face of his father from his nightmares, and he created it to overcome his fear. When Slade and Isabel Rochev realized what Blood had done with the cure, Rochev stabbed him through the chest, killing him for his betrayal.

FACT SHEET

Portrayed by: Graham Shiels
Aliases: Brother Cyrus, the Acolyte
Current Status: deceased
Relationships: none

Comics History: Cyrus Gold is a zombie super-villain named Solomon Grundy in the comics. He has faced off with the entire array of DC Comics' Super Heroes, most notably against Batman.

CYRUS GOLD

Cyrus Gold was one of Brother Blood's most trusted and valued acolytes, and the first test subject to survive Blood's "miracle" serum, otherwise known as mirakuru. He was injected in "State v. Queen" (season 2, episode 7), and although blood poured from his eyes afterward, he survived, gaining superhuman strength, speed, and durability in the process.

Gold had come into Blood's life many years before, at the orphanage where Blood was sent following the death of his father. Gold was a preacher there, and the first person Blood spoke to after a month of silence upon his arrival. Over time, Blood came to view Gold as something akin to an older brother or father figure.

After surviving the mirakuru serum, Gold, now known as the Acolyte, broke into Queen Consolidated's applied sciences division in "The Scientist" (season 2, episode 8) and stole a large-scale centrifuge. The Arrow confronted Gold as he followed up on that heist by stealing blood from a blood bank; Gold was shot in the leg, but escaped. When the Arrow came after him again, this time inside an A.R.G.U.S. bunker, Gold made another getaway, leaving the Arrow unconscious and poisoned.

In "Three Ghosts" (season 2, episode 9) the SCPD come after Gold following a tip from the Arrow. He returned to his apartment to find that the Arrow and Diggle had broken in, but he ferociously attacked them and drove them away. Gold then ambushed the police unit that was trailing them, injuring Quentin Lance and killing Lance's old partner Lucas Hilton.

The Arrow tracked Gold to an abandoned factory and, in the ensuing fight, the Vigilante fired an arrow into the stolen centrifuge, destroying it and sending a spray of chemicals directly into Gold's face, killing him.

"DO NOT HESITATE TO **KILL** CYRUS GOLD, BECAUSE, GIVEN THE **OPPORTUNITY,** HE'LL DO THE **SAME** TO YOU."

HELENA BERTINELLI

Helena Bertinelli is the only daughter of feared Starling City gangster Frank Bertinelli, the man she holds responsible for the death of her fiancé, Michael Staton. Before Staton's death, Helena spent time gathering evidence for the FBI, informing on her father in an effort to punish him for all the evil he had inflicted on the world. But Frank found the laptop containing all her evidence, incorrectly assuming it was Staton's. He had Staton killed to protect his empire, but lost his daughter forever in the process. Taking on the guise of the Huntress, Helena waged a vigilante war on her father's criminal empire, never hesitating to kill anyone who got in her way.

Helena Bertinelli made her first *Arrow* appearance in the episode "Muse of Fire" (season 1, episode 7). Wearing a motorcycle helmet, she gunned down Paul Copani, one of her father's associates, outside Queen Consolidated, almost shooting Moira Queen in the process. Returning home, Helena was asked by her father to have dinner with Oliver to help seal a deal between Frank's construction company and Queen Consolidated. Oliver and Helena enjoyed their dinner despite themselves, and vowed to see each other again soon. Neither could have guessed how soon, however, as both the Hood and the Huntress returned to the restaurant a few minutes later to stop a shakedown attempt by Nick Salvati, another of Frank

Bertinelli's associates. In the process, the Hood was able to remove the helmet covering the Huntress' face, revealing Helena.

Helena and Oliver were then kidnapped by Salvati, who had by then determined that Helena was the Huntress. He threatened to kill Helena the same way he had killed Michael Staton, but Oliver stepped in, and together he and Helena took out Salvati and all of his men. In the *coup de grâce*, Helena snapped Salvati's neck. She realized that Oliver was the Hood, and before long they consummated their relationship, each of them excited by the prospect of being with someone with whom they could be truthful.

In "Vendetta" (season 1, episode 8) Oliver began training Helena in her role as a vigilante, trying to get her to see the difference between justice and revenge. But things went south once more when Helena killed Zhishan, the leader of the Chinese Triad, and made it look like her father was responsible, trying to ignite a gang war. The Hood was able to stop China White and her men from killing Frank, and then stopped Helena as she tried to do the same. Helena refused to forgive Oliver for this, and left town, threatening to reveal his identity if he ever came after her in the future.

The Huntress returned to Starling City in the aptly named "The Huntress Returns" (season 1, episode 17)

FACT SHEET

Portrayed by: Jessica de Gouw
Aliases: the Huntress
Current Status: alive and incarcerated
Relationships: Frank Bertinelli (father, deceased), Michael Staton (fiancé, deceased)

Comics History: The Huntress has a long history as a crossbow-toting vigilante crime-fighter in the comics. She has appeared most often in the Batman family of books, where the Caped Crusader's refusal to kill the bad guys puts him at odds with her "by any means necessary" philosophy. She is also a founding member of the Birds of Prey group with Oracle and Black Canary.

Oliver and Helena were briefly in a relationship, but Helena broke it off after realizing that Oliver was still in love with Laurel.

upon learning that her father planned to cut a deal with the FBI in exchange for a pardon and enrollment in the witness protection program. After killing Frank's lawyer, Helena went to Oliver for help, and when he refused, she attacked Tommy to force Oliver to do as she wished.

Helena attacked the van she believed to be carrying her father, only to discover it was a trap. She got arrested by Quentin Lance, but was quickly rescued by the Hood, who gave her one last chance to leave the city. She of course didn't take it, and went instead to Felicity for help in finding her father's true location. But before Helena could kill her father inside his safe house, Oliver once again stopped her. Their ensuing brawl was interrupted by Detective McKenna Hall, who was intent on arresting

both of them. The Huntress distracted the Hood by shooting McKenna, then slipped away.

Helena came back to Starling City once more in "Birds of Prey" (season 2, episode 17), breaking into the courthouse where Frank Bertinelli was scheduled to go on trial. When she failed to get her hands on her father, she took hostages, including Laurel Lance. Helena then contacted Oliver and offered him a deal: Laurel in exchange for her father. The meet to exchange hostages was interrupted by an overzealous SWAT commander, who intended to take down all the vigilantes present. In the melee, Frank was shot dead by the police and Helena was arrested, despondent that she was not the one who got to kill her father.

"ONCE YOU LET THE **DARKNESS** INSIDE, IT **NEVER** COMES OUT."

"MY FATHER IS A **MONSTER.** HE DOESN'T CARE WHO HE **HURTS** TO KEEP HIS **MONEY AND POWER,** AND I WANTED IT TO **STOP.**"

FACT SHEET

Portrayed by: Jeffrey Nordling
Aliases: none
Current Status: deceased
Relationships: Helena Bertinelli (daughter), Nick Salvati (crime family "son")

Comics History: Frank Bertinelli is based upon the comics character Franco Bertinelli, first appearing in *Batman/Huntress: Cry for Blood* #1. Bertinelli was a major figure in Gotham organized crime, until he was murdered by rival don Stefano Mandragora. His daughter, Helena, survived the hit and went on to become the Huntress.

FRANK BERTINELLI

Frank Bertinelli was a powerful Starling City mafia boss. Not surprisingly, he made a lot of enemies, but the one that caught him by surprise was his daughter, Helena Bertinelli. After he had her fiancé murdered for spying on him for the FBI, Helena vowed to destroy his world the way he had hers.

The Hood saved Frank from his daughter, but he wound up in prison. He made a deal with the FBI to rat out his criminal associates, and was set to go into the witness protection program, when Helena returned and tried to kill him again. Once again, the Hood intervened, and Frank escaped.

In "Birds of Prey" (season 2, episode 17), the Arrow captured Frank Bertinelli and turned him over to the police. Assistant District Attorney Donner set up a fake trial for him in order to lure his daughter out into the open, but Helena was prepared for that and took Laurel Lance hostage inside the courthouse. At Helena's demand, the Arrow abducted Frank to exchange him for Laurel. When Helena was about to kill him, Frank apologized for the hurt he had caused her, saying she had brought him so much joy. She wasn't swayed, but lost her chance to kill him when police captain Harry Stein attacked the vigilantes, killing Frank with a hail of bullets.

FACT SHEET

Portrayed by: Tahmoh Penikett
Aliases: none
Current Status: deceased
Relationships: Frank Bertinelli (boss)
Comics History: Nick Salvati has yet to appear in the comics.

NICK SALVATI

Nick Salvati was Frank Bertinelli's right-hand man and enforcer, appearing in the episode "Muse of Fire" (season 1, episode, 7). While Oliver and Helena were out at dinner, Nick was trying to figure out who was targeting his boss' organization by coming down hard on everyone who owed them protection money. It turned out that one of those was Mr. Russo, the proprietor of the restaurant where Oliver was dining.

Nick and his henchman told Russo that he owed them an extra payment of protection money. They were about to break Russo's fingers when the Hood and the Huntress both burst in, and he fled the scene.

The next day, Nick kidnapped Helena and Oliver and took them to a warehouse to interrogate them. He had already suspected that the killer was someone inside their organization, and the fact that Helena had dropped her necklace at Russo's confirmed this. After beating her, Nick added insult to injury by telling her that he was the one who had murdered her fiancé, on Frank's orders.

He was about to kill Helena too for her betrayal, but Oliver escaped from his ties and attacked him. This started a general brawl, and while Oliver dealt with the other thugs, Helena snapped Nick's neck.

FACT SHEET

Portrayed by: Seth Gabel
Aliases: the Count
Current Status: deceased

Comics History: Werner Vertigo first appeared in the comics as a Star City jewel thief in conflict with Green Arrow and Black Canary. He had a small electronic device implanted in his temple to help compensate for a hereditary inner-ear defect; by tinkering with this device, he was able to affect the balance of others he came into contact with, giving them the sensation of vertigo. At one time or another, Vertigo has been a member of the Injustice Society, the Suicide Squad, and Checkmate.

COUNT VERTIGO

The Count was Starling City's preeminent drug lord, flooding the streets with his deadly designer drug Vertigo. Unfortunately for him, he drew the Hood's attention in "Vertigo" (season 1, episode 12) when Thea Queen was arrested after an automobile accident while under the influence of the narcotic. The Hood hit the streets, looking for revenge.

Oliver used his *bratva* contacts to find the supplier of the drug and arranged a meeting. The meeting was broken up by the police, however, but not before the Count dosed Oliver with Vertigo. Diggle was able to get Oliver back to the Arrowcave in time to treat him with medicinal herbs from the island to fight the drug's effects. Oliver was then able to analyze the substance, tracking down its ingredients to find the Count. This time, Oliver injected him with the drug, in a dose strong enough to break his mind. The Count was declared insane and placed in a mental institution.

But he recovered from his overdose and was transferred to Iron Heights, the maximum-security prison in the Glades. He escaped along with several others when the Undertaking's earthquake rocked the facility, and returned to the streets six months later, now known as Count Vertigo. This time, he was out to do more than just make money; he was able to poison a large portion of the city by using flu vaccination stations. Felicity Smoak was able to deduce his dastardly delivery method, and when she came to investigate, he took her hostage. Count Vertigo was then able to do some deductive reasoning of his own, and figured that Oliver Queen must be the Arrow, given the Felicity connection. He then called Oliver's office to let him know he had Felicity. The Arrow showed up and tried reasoning with Count Vertigo, but when that didn't work, he put three arrows in the villain's chest, sending him stumbling out through a window and crashing into a car below, dead.

"YOU KNOW **WHY** THEY CALL HIM THE COUNT? WHEN HE WAS DEVELOPING THIS **DRUG,** HE **EXPERIMENTED** ON THE HOMELESS, PROSTITUTES, RUNAWAYS. THE POLICE WOULD FIND THEIR **BODIES,** PUNCTURE **MARKS** ON THEIR NECK, LIKE A **VAMPIRE.**"

When the Hood injected him with massive amounts of the drug Vertigo, the Count was declared insane and incarcerated in a mental hospital. He escaped during the Undertaking, however, returning as Count Vertigo. He soon spread his poison throughout Starling City.

"EVERYBODY LOVES A PRETTY DOLL."

BARTON MATHIS

Barton Mathis (aka "the Dollmaker") made a particularly dark appearance in "Broken Dolls" (season 2, episode 3). Mathis was a sadistic serial killer put away years before by Detective Lance, only to escape from Iron Heights prison during the Undertaking that destroyed the Glades.

Given his personal connection to the case, Lance was forced to the sidelines for the investigation of Mathis' subsequent killing spree, leaving him no choice but to reach out to the Arrow for help. Lance and the Arrow teamed up to break into a police lab containing evidence from the case, and discovered the link between all the victims.

Felicity Smoak offered herself as bait so Oliver, Diggle, and Lance could catch Mathis, but he went on the offensive and abducted both Quentin and Laurel Lance, before being stopped by the Arrow and captured before he was able to kill them. He was then killed by a mysterious new female vigilante—later revealed to be Sara Lance, the Canary—who was none too pleased about what the Dollmaker had tried to do to her sister.

FACT SHEET

Portrayed by: Andrew Dunbar
Aliases: Firefly
Current Status: deceased
Relationships: unnamed wife and children

Comics History: Firefly is a pyromaniac super-villain in the comics, often battling with Batman and his allies. He began his crime career as a protégé of Killer Moth, as the pair looked to distort and duplicate the success of the relationship between Batman and Robin.

GARFIELD LYNNS

Garfield Lynns burst onto the scene in "Burned" (season 1, episode 10). When two Starling City firefighters were killed in the line of duty, Laurel Lance suspected foul play and contacted the Vigilante for assistance. Oliver tracked the murders to Garfield Lynns, a SCFD firefighter believed to have died in a massive blaze several years before. Lynns, however, survived the fire, albeit with severe burns over his entire body.

Lynns showed up at a charity event for firefighters, intent on gaining revenge against the fire chief who had not sent back-up the night Lynns was almost fatally burnt. Luckily, Oliver Queen was in attendance (he was hosting it, in fact, at his nightclub) and was able to save the chief in the guise of the Vigilante. His quest for vengeance thwarted, Lynns committed suicide by lighting himself on fire.

"TIMING IS EVERYTHING."

FACT SHEET

Portrayed by: Robert Knepper
Aliases: the Clock King
Current Status: alive and incarcerated
Relationships: unknown

Comics History: Clock King has tangled numerous times with Green Arrow in the comics, and at various times has been a member of the Injustice League and the Suicide Squad.

WILLIAM TOCKMAN

The Clock King made his first appearance in "Time of Death" (season 2, episode 14). William Tockman was a low-level criminal operator who masterminded a perfectly timed robbery at Kord Industries, making off with an electronic device that would allow him to access any bank vault in the world. He then set his sights on several within Starling City, but the Arrow and Black Canary stopped his next robbery.

In response, Tockman hacked into the computer server in the Arrow's secret hideout, overloading them so that they exploded. Felicity then enacted a plan to bait Tockman into one last heist. He shot her and almost got away, but Felicity used Tockman's own computer virus to make his cell phone explode, knocking him out, after which he was captured and sent to Iron Heights.

FACT SHEET

Portrayed by: Christopher Redman

Aliases: the Savior

Current Status: deceased

Relationships: Emma Falk (wife, deceased)

Comics History: The Savior has yet to appear in the comics.

"I FIND YOU GUILTY."

JOSEPH FALK

The Savior brought his own brand of justice in the episode "Salvation." He appeared to be a copycat vigilante, inspired by the Hood's one-man war against corruption and abuse, and served as a dark mirror for Oliver to view the reflection of his own actions. The Savior kidnaped a slumlord who had recently avoided criminal prosecution by paying off the district attorney. The Savior forced the man to confess his atrocities over a live Internet broadcast, and then executed him in front of a spellbound audience.

Falk then shifted his attention to the district attorney. While trying to track the signal for this broadcast, Felicity realized that the signal kept moving, and Oliver was too late to save the DA.

The Savior went after Roy Harper next, since he viewed him as just another petty criminal. But Diggle used a tracking map of the signal to determine that the Savior was using an abandoned subway car to travel around the city, which allowed Oliver to catch up to them and stop the Savior just as he was about to execute Roy.

FACT SHEET

Portrayed by: Currie Graham (Derek Reston), Sarah-Jane Redmond (Alice Reston), Kyle Schmid (Kyle Reston), Tom Stevens (Teddy Reston)

Aliases: the Royal Flush Gang: Ace, King, Queen, Jack

Current Status: King is deceased; the rest are alive and incarcerated

Relationships: each other

Comics History: The Royal Flush Gang first appeared in *Justice League of America* #43 in 1966. Originally just the five clubs that make up a royal flush, the organization has since expanded to include the other suits in a deck of cards, giving them the reach and influence to rival Intergang.

ROYAL FLUSH GANG

The Royal Flush Gang made their first *Arrow* appearance in "Legacies" (season 1, episode 6). Their case proved to be a turning point in Oliver Queen's fledging career as a vigilante, as Diggle was able to convince Oliver to expand his work beyond his father's list and help the police apprehend a gang of bank robbers who were terrorizing Starling City.

With Felicity Smoak's assistance, Oliver was able to use police files to determine that the gang was actually the Reston family: Derek (King), Alice (Queen), and their sons: Kyle (Ace) and Teddy (Jack). Derek Reston was a former Queen Consolidated employee who lost his job when Robert Queen outsourced 1,500 jobs to China. Oliver felt great guilt over this, and attempted to reason with Derek to right his own wrongs. But it didn't work, and the Gang attempted to rob another bank. During this confrontation, Derek was shot and killed, and another wedge was driven between Oliver and his memory of his own father.

"YOU **SHOT** A **COP**!"

"YOU KNOW HOW OUR BROTHERHOOD WORKS: I DO A FAVOR FOR YOU, AND YOU DO ONE FOR ME."

ALEXI LEONOV

Alexi Leonov was a member of *bratva*, the Russian mafia, who operated under the cover of an auto body shop. Oliver Queen met Leonov in "Lone Gunmen" (season 1, episode 3), using his connections with high-ranking *bratva* member Anatoly Knyazev to initiate a relationship with the mobster. Oliver asked Leonov to identify the assassin Deadshot, and he came through, revealing the killer's name was Floyd Lawton.

In "Vertigo" (season 1, episode 12) Leonov arranged a meeting between Oliver and the Count, but not before he had tested Oliver's *bratva* loyalty. He demanded that Oliver kill a beaten man who had done something Leonov had

told him not to do. Oliver made it look like he choked the man to death, but later revived him.

In "Suicide Squad" (season 2, episode 16), Oliver asked Leonov to find out where Slade Wilson was staying in Starling City. Leonov wanted a favor in return, and Oliver agreed, but when Leonov demanded Oliver do something for him first, Oliver lost his patience and injured two of Leonov's thugs to indicate who the boss in this situation was. Leonov got him the information he wanted, but told Oliver that he was through working with him. Oliver followed the lead to Slade's office, only to find Alexi Leonov dead in Slade's chair, an arrow through his eye.

FACT SHEET

Portrayed by: Eugene Lipinski
Aliases: none
Current Status: deceased
Relationships: Oliver Queen (associate)

Comics History: Alexi Leonov has yet to appear in the comics.

"I'M EXACTLY LIKE YOU; I ONLY STEAL FROM THE RICH."

FACT SHEET

Portrayed by: James Callis

Aliases: the Dodger (real name unknown)

Current Status: incarcerated

Relationships: Cass Derenick (associate), Claire Abbott (associate)

Comics History: The Dodger has yet to appear in the comics.

THE DODGER

The Dodger was an elusive international thief, so named because he avoided getting his own hands dirty, instead using hostages to do his stealing for him. His signature move was putting an explosive collar around his hostage's neck, and then if they didn't steal what he wanted them to, he'd blow their head off.

He had a particular fondness for antiquities from the Ominous Decade (the last ten years of King Ferdinand of Spain's reign), so Team Arrow set a trap for him using Oliver's family jewels. He took the bait faster than expected, and when Felicity Smoak tried to stop him, he placed a bomb collar around her neck. The Dodger couldn't dodge all of the Hood's moves, however, and wound up at the receiving end of his other signature weapon, a stun baton.

FACT SHEET

Portrayed by: J. August Richards

Aliases: Mr. Blank (real name unknown)

Current Status: deceased

Relationships: Edward Rasmus (employer)

Comics History: Mr. Blank has yet to appear in the comics.

"SUCH **PAIN** HERE. A SENSE OF **LOSS** AND **REGRET.** YOU CAN FEEL IT, **DOWN** TO THE WOOD **PANELING.**"

MR. BLANK

Mr. Blank was an assassin hired by Edward Rasmus to kill the Moore family, who were suing Rasmus for stealing their life savings. Blank killed Eric and Nancy Moore, but their son Taylor escaped. He saw the killer's face, so Mr. Blank went after him again, this time in Laurel Lance's apartment. Fortunately, Laurel knew how to defend herself, and when the Hood joined in the fight, Mr. Blank cut his losses and dove out of a window.

Rattled by the Hood, Rasmus confessed to the police that he was behind the Moore murders, and that he had told Mr. Blank to forget about Taylor Moore. But Mr. Blank couldn't abide anyone seeing his face, and refused to walk away from the job, even going so far as to kill his employer, who had made the mistake of arranging a face-to-face meeting with Mr. Blank in prison.

He tracked Taylor to the Queen mansion, but in attacking Oliver Queen he unknowingly went up against the Hood, and lost. Oliver killed Mr. Blank with a chimney poker, but gave the credit to a nearby dead security guard.

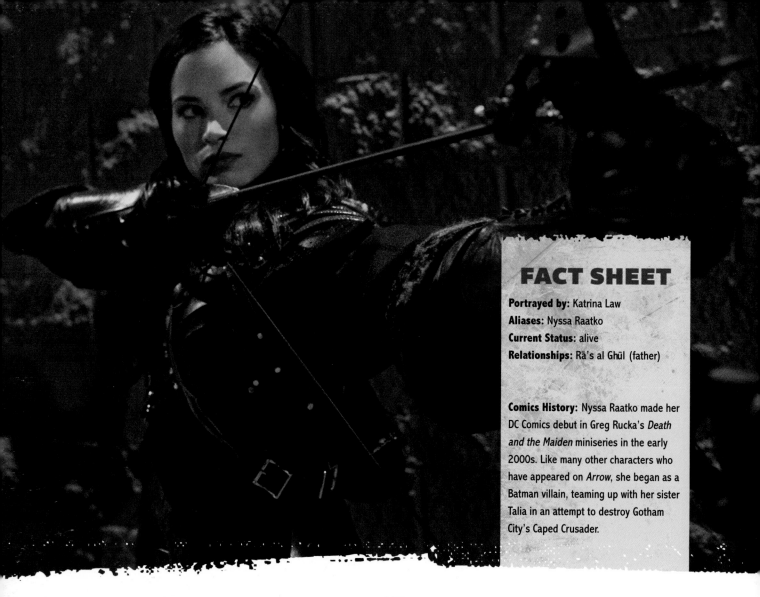

FACT SHEET

Portrayed by: Katrina Law
Aliases: Nyssa Raatko
Current Status: alive
Relationships: Rā's al Ghūl (father)

Comics History: Nyssa Raatko made her DC Comics debut in Greg Rucka's *Death and the Maiden* miniseries in the early 2000s. Like many other characters who have appeared on *Arrow*, she began as a Batman villain, teaming up with her sister Talia in an attempt to destroy Gotham City's Caped Crusader.

NYSSA AL GHŪL

Nyssa al Ghūl is the daughter of Rā's al Ghūl, and a member of the League of Assassins. When Sara Lance was swept away from the *Amazo* off the coast of Lian Yu, Nyssa found her and nursed her back to health in Nanda Parbat, the League's headquarters. Sara was granted membership, and she and Nyssa became lovers.

In "Heir to the Demon" (season 2, episode 13) Nyssa arrived in Starling City looking for Sara, seeking to force her to return to Nanda Parbat. Sara begged for Nyssa to release her from the League, but Nyssa wasn't hearing it, angry and hurt that Sara had left without saying goodbye.

The League kidnapped Sara's mother, Dinah Lance, and gave Sara an ultimatum: she had 24 hours to return to Nanda Parbat or Dinah would die. Instead, Sara ingested poison, and then told Nyssa she would rejoin the League. As Nyssa kept her word and released Dinah, Sara revealed that she would be dead in mere minutes.

An enraged Nyssa then attempted to kill both Dinah and Quentin Lance, only to be stopped by the Arrow. A weakened Sara begged the Arrow not to kill Nyssa; he spared her, then saved Sara with herbs from Lian Yu. Moved by all she had seen, Nyssa released Sara from her League obligations.

Nyssa and the League of Assassins returned to Starling City in the season 2 finale "Unthinkable" (season 2, episode 23). After disappearing a few days prior, Sara returned to the city with the League in tow, giving the Arrow and his allies the reinforcements they needed to turn the tide against Slade Wilson's mirakuru army. Nyssa herself delivered the deathblow to Isabel Rochev, in direct defiance of Oliver's demand for no fatalities. In return for their help, Sara once again left Starling City, this time on a boat bound for Nanda Parbat, having rejoined Nyssa and the League of Assassins.

"THE **ONLY** REASON YOU'RE **ALIVE** TODAY IS BECAUSE OF **ME**."

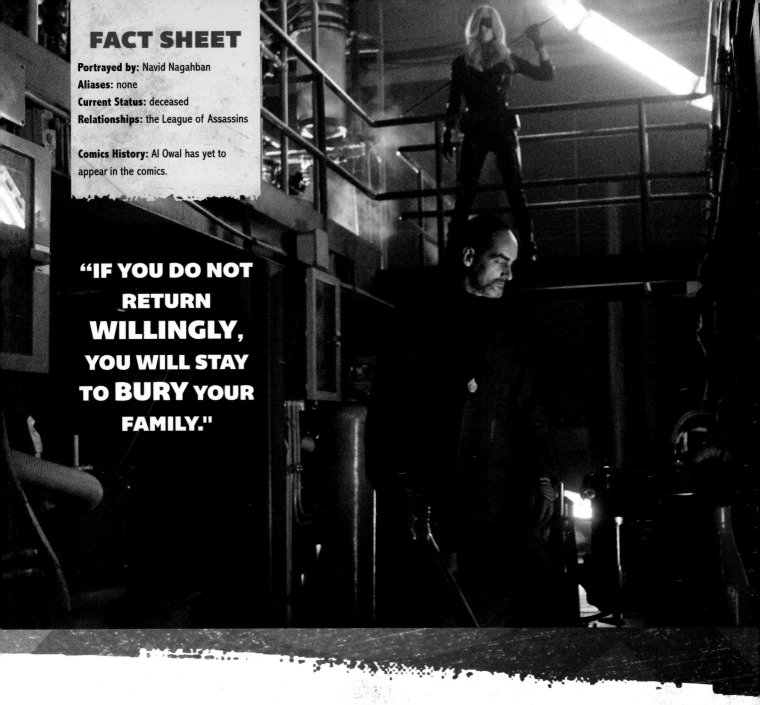

"IF YOU DO NOT RETURN WILLINGLY, YOU WILL STAY TO BURY YOUR FAMILY."

AL OWAL

Al Owal was a prominent member of the League of Assassins. In the episode "League of Assassins" (season 2, episode 5) he led two other assassins to Starling City to capture Sara Lance and bring her back to Nanda Parbat to face Rā's al Ghūl and answer for her desertion.

Al Owal broke into Queen Mansion and battled Sara and Oliver to a standstill. Using a soil sample he left behind, Felicity tracked the assassin back to an old pesticide factory they were using as a base of operations. Sara and Oliver found him there, where he was joined by the other two assassins, and they fought to another stalemate. This time, Al Owal threatened to kill Sara's family. He also revealed that he was the man who trained Malcolm Merlyn when he served with the League of Assassins.

The battle resumed at Sara's clock-tower hideout, the assassins attacking when Sara was alone with her father. But the Arrow arrived soon thereafter, and the three heroes fought off the assassins. Lance shot and killed one, then Sara snapped Al Owal's neck and told the remaining assassin to warn Rā's al Ghūl to stay away from her family.

CHIEN NA WEI

Chien Na Wei is the Chinese Triad's top assassin. Under the training and tutelage of the man responsible for killing her parents, Zhishan, Chien became known as China White, whose deadly pair of karambit knives are feared throughout the city.

China White first appeared on *Arrow* in "Honor Thy Father" (season 1, episode 2), when she was contracted by Martin Somers to kill Laurel Lance. Laurel had filed a civil suit against Somers for his involvement with the Triad drug trade. The Hood was able to save Laurel, going toe to toe with China White before the police arrived and forced them both to flee.

Helena Bertinelli killed Zhishan in "Vendetta" (season 1, episode 8), then convinced the Triad that her gangster father, Frank Bertinelli, was behind it in an effort to provoke an all-out gang war. China White took the death of her mentor personally and led her troops to Bertinelli's home, intending to kill everyone there. She took out

many of Bertinelli's crew, but then the Hood arrived and shot her in the leg, although she managed to escape alive.

China White resurfaced in "Dodger" (season 1, episode 15), meeting with Moira Queen for a job to kill Malcolm Merlyn. China White decided to bring in a professional hitman for the job, going first to Guillermo Barrera (only to have him killed by the Hood), and then to Deadshot. He and China White nearly got to Merlyn, killing several members of his security team before the Hood once again stopped her.

Following the Undertaking, China White found a willing new partner in the Bronze Tiger. In "Identity" (season 2, episode 2) the pair worked a scheme in which they hijacked medical supplies meant for the struggling Glades Memorial Hospital and sold them on the black market. But the Arrow brought in a new partner as well, Roy Harper, and this time China White did not escape; she was apprehended and taken into police custody.

FACT SHEET

Portrayed by: Kelly Hu

Aliases: China White

Current Status: alive and incarcerated

Relationships: parents (deceased), Zhishan (father figure, deceased)

Comics History: Chien Na Wei has yet to appear in the comics.

THE LIST

As *Arrow* began, Oliver Queen returned from Lian Yu with a mission: to eliminate or otherwise neutralize the people on a list of names given to him by his father in his dying moments. The list consisted of a multitude of Starling City's top moneymakers, business executives who had feasted on the misfortunes of the city's downtrodden for too long, and the gangsters who were in league with them. For the better part of the first season, Oliver focused on them, one by one.

GUILLERMO BARRERA

Guillermo Barrera was a hitman hired by China White to kill Malcolm Merlyn for Moira Queen in "Dead to Rights" (season 1, episode 16). Upon his arrival in Starling City, he was met at the airport by the Hood, who killed him after a brief, brutal fight.

JASON BRODEUR

Jason Brodeur was the CEO of Brodeur Chemical, a shady company engaged in the illegal dumping of toxic waste. One of his employees blew the whistle on Brodeur, who in return had her killed, and her husband, Peter Declan, framed for it, in "An Innocent Man" (season 1, episode 4). The Hood worked closely with Laurel Lance to prove Declan's innocence and Brodeur's guilt.

TED GAYNOR

Ted Gaynor was Diggle's commanding officer in Afghanistan before hooking up with Blackhawk Squad Protection Group, a private contractor. Upon their return home, Gaynor led the Blackhawks in numerous robberies in "Trust But Verify" (season 1, episode 11) before catching an arrow in the chest from the Hood.

JAMES HOLDER

James Holder became the Hood's target in "Lone Gunmen" (season 1, episode 3) after several deaths occurred in low-income housing thanks to Holder's defective smoke detectors. But before the Hood could get to him, Holder was shot and killed by Deadshot at the behest of Warren Patel, as Holder was interested in purchasing the same company as Patel.

ADAM HUNT

Adam Hunt was the CEO of Hunt Multinational, and a ruthless and ill-tempered man. After being threatened by the Hood in "Pilot" (season 1, episode 1), Hunt didn't back down, and as a result had his bank accounts hacked, the money being transferred to his victims. Hunt tried to make a financial comeback in "Year's End" (season 1, episode 9), only to be murdered by the Dark Archer in an attempt to draw out the Hood.

DOUGLAS MILLER

Dr. Douglas Miller is the head of the Queen Consolidated applied sciences division. He made the List thanks to his second job: secretly working for the diabolical Malcolm Merlyn, helping to design the machinery needed for the Undertaking to destroy the Glades.

THE FUTURE OF THE LIST

When Oliver was on Lian Yu, he ripped out and burned what he thought was a blank page of his father's notebook. He soon discovered that the book contained the List, written in invisible ink. Upon his return to Starling City, he put the book to good use, but what if that page he burned had contained something of great significance? "Actually, I sort of half-jokingly say that that page contained all the details of the Undertaking," confides executive producer Marc Guggenheim. "There are reasonable questions like, 'Well, if Oliver had access to his father's book, why didn't he know this? Why didn't he know that?' So, for my money, all the answers to those questions can be backed up by, 'Well, they were all on that page that he burned.'"

Oliver stopped using the List in the aftermath of the Undertaking, but there's no reason he couldn't go back to it. After all, the names on the List are still people involved with criminal activity, so it's not out of the question, as Guggenheim confirms. "I think it would feel like we were regressing if we did an episode where Oliver just opens the book to a page and goes after a guy on the List. But we like the idea of returning to the book... and we have a couple of different notions as to how to do that."

LEO MUELLER

Leo Mueller was a German arms dealer trying to make a living in Starling City before the Hood put an end to it in "Damaged" (season 1, episode 5), shooting an arrow through his chest.

JOHN NICKEL

John Nickel was a Glades slumlord. He was kidnapped and murdered by the Savior in "Salvation" (season 1, episode 18). The Savior browbeat a confession out of Nickel, broadcasting it live on the Internet, and then killing him.

NELSON RAVICH

Nelson Ravich was an embezzler who returned the $70 million he had stolen after a brief "conversation" with the Hood in "Year's End" (season 1, episode 9). He was then killed by the Dark Archer.

MARCUS REDMAN

Marcus Redman was another embezzler who had a change of heart, returning $30 million to the Halcyon pension plan after a meeting with the Hood in "Honor Thy Father" (season 1, episode 2).

MARTIN SOMERS

Martin Somers was the CEO of Starling Port, and had ties to the drug trade through the Chinese Triad. When Laurel Lance filed a civil suit faulting Somers for the death of her client's father in "Honor Thy Father" (season 1, episode 2), the Triad sent the assassin China White to silence her. But the Hood saved Laurel, and then forced a confession from Somers, leading to his arrest.

ANTHONY VENZA

Anthony Venza was a drug dealer with ties to the Bertinelli crime family. He was taken down by the Hood and the Huntress in "Vendetta" (season 1, episode 8) and left for the police to arrest.

KEN WILLIAMS

Williams stole millions of dollars from his clients in a pyramid scheme. The Hood seemed likely to put an arrow through his chest in "Dodger" (season 1, episode 15), before an argument with Felicity over his methods led to him leaving Williams (a father and little league coach) alive.

SUICIDE SQUAD

The Suicide Squad is a team of convicts forced to work for A.R.G.U.S., led by the indomitable Amanda Waller. Its official name is Task Force X, but this is rarely used by the members of the squad themselves, considering the extremely dangerous (even suicidal) missions they are sent on. Their reward for completing them is reduced jail sentences. To ensure their cooperation, each member has a micro-bomb implanted in their bodies.

Six members have been revealed so far: previous *Arrow* antagonists Bronze Tiger, Deadshot, and Shrapnel; newcomers Ravan and Torque (played by Viv Leacock and Michael Adamthwaite); and longtime DC Comics villain Harley Quinn (voiced by Tara Strong). John Diggle and Lyla Michaels were also part of the Suicide Squad for a time.

> "THIS AIN'T NO TASK FORCE. LET'S CALL IT LIKE IT IS. WELCOME TO THE SUICIDE SQUAD."

AMANDA WALLER

Amanda Waller is the cold, calculating special agent in charge of A.R.G.U.S., a shadowy government agency that uses shadowy tactics to protect shadowy interests from shadowy characters. Fittingly, Waller was a shadowy figure on *Arrow* long before viewers ever saw her face; she maintained radio contact with Edward Fyers on Lian Yu during season 1 flashbacks to Oliver's time on the island, seeking out Yao Fei. It seemed that Fyers was working for her, helping to redirect cargo headed for China, disrupting trade there in an attempt to destabilize the Chinese economy. The plan failed, however, as Oliver Queen and Slade Wilson got involved, killing Fyers and all of his men.

Waller returned for season 2, this time in person. In "Keep Your Enemies Closer" (season 2, episode 6) she captured John Diggle in an effort to gain his help in rescuing his ex-wife (and A.R.G.U.S. agent) Lyla Michaels, who was somewhere in Russia. Amanda turned the screws on Diggle in this meeting, telling him in no uncertain terms that A.R.G.U.S. was very aware of how he and Oliver spent their nights.

Waller then began putting together a group of criminals she deemed expendable to send on impossible missions no one else was skilled enough to carry out. Officially, she called the group Task Force X, but others called it the Suicide Squad. Following a mission in Markovia led by Lyla and Diggle, Oliver Queen visited Waller in her office for a conversation that made it clear they both knew Slade Wilson, and believed him to be dead. Waller then showed Oliver an A.R.G.U.S. file on a new mercenary they'd codenamed "Deathstroke," a man she believed could be Slade Wilson.

FACT SHEET

Portrayed by: Cynthia Addai-Robinson
Aliases: the Wall, Mockingbird
Current Status: alive
Relationships: classified

Comics History: Amanda Waller is a
highly placed, mysterious government
operative in the comics, and has held top
leadership positions in both Checkmate
and Task Force X, where she oversaw
the Suicide Squad. She also held a
cabinet-level position as Secretary of
Metahuman Affairs in President Lex
Luthor's administration.

"WHO DO YOU WANT TO KILL MORE THAN ME?"

"SO THIS IS YOUR UNIT, HUH, WALLER? WHAT, O.J. AND CHARLES MANSON WEREN'T AVAILABLE?"

Ruthless to the point of callousness, there is no doubt that when something needs doing, Amanda Waller gets results.

Waller returned during Slade Wilson's mirakuru army's assault on Starling City. Her A.R.G.U.S. agents moved in quickly to bottle up the city, blocking all avenues out of town in an effort to contain Wilson's soldiers. As a not-so-last resort, she called in a drone strike, willing to sacrifice the half-million citizens of Starling City to save the hundreds of millions she thought would be lost should Wilson's army succeed.

But Diggle, Lyla, and Deadshot were able to keep her in check long enough for the Arrow and the Canary to stop Wilson's army on their own, thereby avoiding what would have been a horrible catastrophe.

FACT SHEET

Portrayed by: Michael Rowe
Aliases: Floyd Lawton
Current Status: alive
Relationships: Chloe Lawton (daughter)

Comics History: Deadshot is a popular villain in the comics, a hired assassin skilled in the use of a wide variety of weapons. He made his first appearances in Gotham City in an unsuccessful attempt to replace Batman. He has since been a member of the Suicide Squad and a regular in the Secret Six.

DEADSHOT

Floyd Lawton, better known as Deadshot, is the *Arrow* universe's foremost assassin, motivated by one thing: a love of money. Everything he does is for financial gain—he even passed up an opportunity to kill his arch nemesis John Diggle on the off-chance that someone might pay him to do it later.

Deadshot was the first masked villain from the comics to make an appearance on *Arrow* (although, of course, he didn't wear a mask on the show), debuting in "Lone Gunmen" (season 1, episode 3). He appeared in Starling City and beat the Hood to James Holder, killing one of the first men on Robert Queen's list before Oliver got a chance. Oliver used his *bratva* connections to track the poisoned bullet Deadshot used to an apartment registered to someone called Floyd Lawton. Lawton escaped, but then reappeared for an attempt to kill Walter Steele, Oliver's stepfather and the CEO of Queen

Consolidated. The Hood shot an arrow through Lawton's eye. As he staggered out of the building, Deadshot was taken away by a mysterious group of men in a van.

Sometime before the events depicted in *Arrow*, Lawton was responsible for the murder of John Diggle's brother Andy; as a result, Diggle vowed that he would be the one to bring Lawton to justice, by whatever means necessary. Lawton's body is covered with tattoos of the names of all his victims, and he has a blank space next to Andy Diggle's name that he said he was saving for John.

Deadshot returned in "Dead to Rights" (season 1, episode 16). Now retired due to his eye injury, he was approached by Triad assassin China White, who offered him a cybernetic eye in exchange for killing Malcolm Merlyn. Lawton agreed, and worked with White to attack Malcolm in his office building. Lawton was able to shoot Malcolm several times, poisoning him with curare bullets,

"SO… WHO NEEDS **TWO BULLETS** IN THE **CHEST?**"

but Malcolm survived after the Hood helped Tommy Merlyn give his father a blood transfusion.

"Keep Your Enemies Closer" (season 2, episode 6) revealed that Deadshot had been captured and was being held in a Russian gulag. In an effort to rescue his ex-wife Lyla Michaels—who had herself traveled to Russia following Deadshot's trail—Diggle got himself locked up in the prison, thanks to Oliver's *bratva* comrades. Diggle found Lawton locked in an isolation freezer, but freed him in exchange for help with rescuing Lyla. In return for Diggle allowing him to walk away, Lawton revealed that he had been contracted by H.I.V.E. to kill Andy Diggle.

In "Suicide Squad" (season 2, episode 16) Diggle learned that Deadshot had been apprehended by A.R.G.U.S., and was forced to team with him and other expendable convicts on a mission to stop an Afghan terrorist in Markovia from selling nerve gas to the highest bidder. In this episode, Deadshot revealed that he has a young daughter named Zoe, and that the money he earned was placed in a blind trust for her.

Deadshot was last seen at the end of season 2, when Diggle and Lyla broke him out of his prison cell to help them stop Amanda Waller from unleashing a drone attack on Starling City.

"NO KILL SHOTS? I WAS PROMISED A FIGHT!"

FACT SHEET

Portrayed by: Michael Jai White
Aliases: Bronze Tiger
Current Status: alive and incarcerated
Relationships: unknown

Comics History: Bronze Tiger has a long history in the comics, making his first appearance in *Richard Dragon, Kung Fu Fighter* #1 in 1975. Bronze Tiger, one of the greatest martial artists in the world, has been a hero and villain since, and allied with Batman. He has been a member of both the League of Assassins and the Suicide Squad.

BEN TURNER

Ben Turner (aka Bronze Tiger) wears a pair of long metal claws, which he uses to swipe at enemies and swat aside projectiles, such as the Hood's arrows. The claws resemble *tekko-kagi*, common among ninja warriors of Japan.

Bronze Tiger first appeared in "Identity" (season 2, episode 2). He teamed up with Triad assassin China White, agreeing to help her raid medical supply transport trucks in exchange for the opportunity to fight and kill the Hood. The Hood battled Tiger and China White at every turn, finally stopping Bronze Tiger the third time they fought with an electric arrow that left Turner incapacitated and incarcerated.

Turner was broken out of prison in "Tremors" (season 2, episode 12) by arms dealer Milo Armitage, who paid him $10 million to steal a prototype of Malcolm Merlyn's earthquake machine from the Merlyn mansion. He was stopped by the Hood and Roy Harper, who returned him to prison, where he was approached by Amanda Waller with a suicide-strings-attached offer to get out of jail.

"Suicide Squad" (season 2, episode 16) saw Bronze Tiger team up with Deadshot, Shrapnel, Lyla Michaels, and John Diggle to stop Gholem Qadir from selling nerve gas to the highest bidder. Turner killed Qadir before the terrorist could kill Lyla, earning him some brownie points, but not enough to get him out of jail.

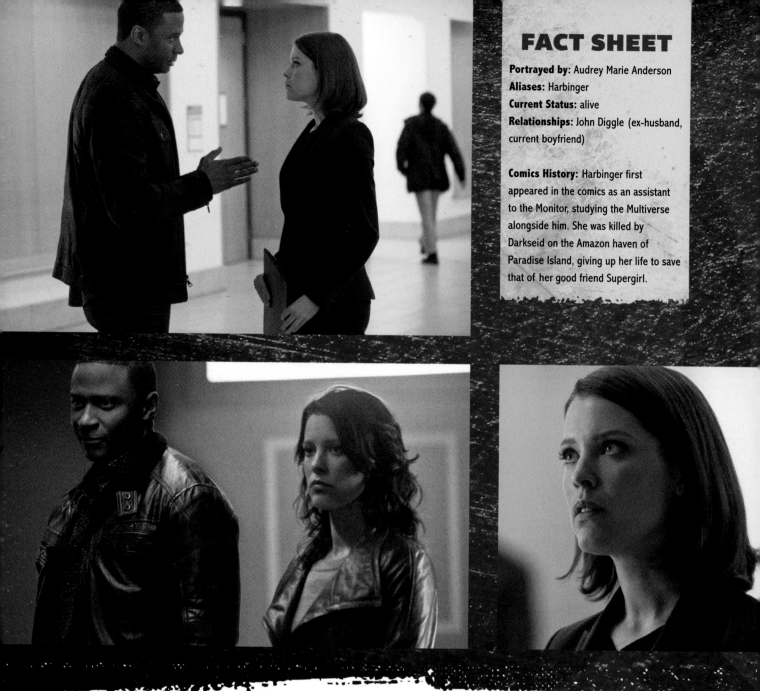

FACT SHEET

Portrayed by: Audrey Marie Anderson
Aliases: Harbinger
Current Status: alive
Relationships: John Diggle (ex-husband, current boyfriend)

Comics History: Harbinger first appeared in the comics as an assistant to the Monitor, studying the Multiverse alongside him. She was killed by Darkseid on the Amazon haven of Paradise Island, giving up her life to save that of her good friend Supergirl.

LYLA MICHAELS

Lyla Michaels is a high-ranking A.R.G.U.S. special agent with field command of Task Force X, also known as the Suicide Squad. She's also the ex-partner, ex-wife, and current girlfriend of John Diggle.

Lyla met Diggle in Afghanistan, where they both saw combat. They were soon married, but their return to the States following Diggle's second tour was too much for their marriage; they couldn't handle peacetime, and were soon divorced. John headed back to the desert for a third tour of duty, and Lyla signed on with A.R.G.U.S.

Lyla appeared in several episodes in the first season of *Arrow*, as Diggle attempted to use her connections and intel to help him track down Deadshot, his brother's killer. The couple drew closer in the second season, and renewed the romantic side of their relationship, in between Suicide Squad missions and months-long sojourns to Russian gulags.

Lyla's boss, Amanda Waller, provided one of the season 2 finale's most shocking moments when she told Diggle that Lyla was pregnant.

"I WILL NOT LET YOU USE MY AGENCY TO SETTLE YOUR BLOOD FEUD."

"TOO LONG HAVE THE PEOPLE OF THIS CITY SUFFERED UNDER THE SHACKLES OF A CORRUPT GOVERNMENT. SLAVES TO SELF-INTERESTED POLITICIANS AND THEIR LOBBYIST PUPPETEERS. I DECLARE WAR ON THEM ALL."

MARK SCHEFFER

Mark Scheffer was a crazed serial bomber with strong anti-government leanings who orchestrated a series of explosions around the city, earning him the moniker Shrapnel. He first appeared in "Blast Radius" (season 2, episode 10). When Councilman Sebastian Blood kicked off his campaign for mayor with a unity rally for the city, Scheffer found the perfect target. But the Hood arrived just in time, and apprehended Scheffer.

Shrapnel returned in "Suicide Squad" (season 2, episode 16) as a member of Amanda Waller's expendable task force, working with Deadshot, Bronze Tiger, Harbinger, and Diggle on the team's mission to take down Afghani terrorist Gholem Qadir. However, Scheffer disobeyed orders and attempted to escape, so Waller made an example of him, detonating the bomb A.R.G.U.S. had implanted inside his body.

FACT SHEET

Portrayed by: Sean Maher
Aliases: Shrapnel
Current Status: deceased
Relationships: unknown

Comics History: Shrapnel is a much
more literal *nom de guerre* in the comics,
as the Mark Scheffer there has a body
made of hundreds of pieces of a metallic
substance, each one a living organism
controlled by his consciousness.
Shrapnel literally explodes, the pieces of
his body directed and recalled at will.

SPECIAL THANKS

Greg Berlanti, Marc Guggenheim, Andrew Kreisberg, Carl Ogawa, Wendy Mericle, Beth Schwartz, Laura Hanson, Cindi Marks, Steve Fogelson,

Dominique Borno, Jill Righton, Lisa Fitzpatrick, Elaine Piechowski, Josh Anderson, Stephanie Mente.

Egg carton baubles

1 Cut two sections from an egg carton.

2 Make a hole through the bottom of each section and pull a thread with a knot in the end through both (so you can hang the bauble up). You could use a bead instead of a knot.

3 Glue the two parts together.

4 Paint with poster paint and decorate with glitter, beads or sequins.

5 Hang up singly or link several.

Matchbox baubles

1 Place a small present in the tray of a matchbox, e.g. a few small coins (a cent, if you're poor; $2, if you're rich!), some lollies, a tiny toy or model, a trinket or two.

2 Cover the matchbox with pretty wrapping paper (or use coloured paper decorated with glitter).

3 Tie to the tree.

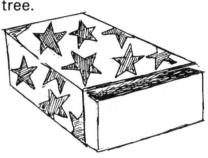

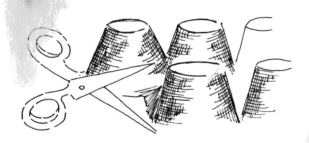

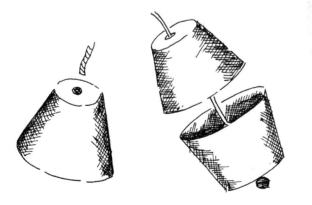

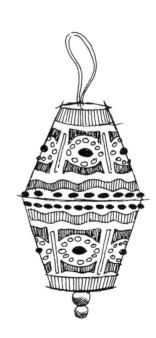

Biscuits and Shortbread

Iced biscuits

You will need:

250g plain flour
125g butter
125g brown sugar
1 egg, beaten
pinch of salt

1 Beat butter and sugar together until fluffy.

2 Mix in the egg a little at a time.

3 Sift in flour and salt. Mix well.

4 Roll out dough on floured board to 1/2cm thickness.

5 Cut into Christmas shapes with cutters.

6 Cook biscuits on greased trays in oven at 190°C, for about 15 minutes.

7 Ice and decorate. You can make icing by mixing icing sugar and hot water together until smooth, then adding drops of food colouring.

Christmas shortbread

You will need:

    150g plain flour
    100g butter
     50g sugar

1 Sift sugar and flour into a mixing bowl.

2 Rub butter into flour and sugar until it looks something like breadcrumbs.

3 Roll the dough into a ball.

4 Take a piece of the dough and roll it into a squared finger shape. Flatten it gently with a fork. (Make it about 1cm thick.)

5 Place finished shortbread fingers on a greased baking tray and cook in the oven at 170°C for 20 minutes.

6 Turn the oven down to 150°C and continue cooking for another 20-25 minutes, until golden brown.

7 Cool.

Bon-Bons

These cost the earth in the shops and we always find them very disappointing!
Try making some better ones of your own.

1 Make a paper tube.

2 Cut through nearly all of the middle of the tube (to make it easier to pull apart). Leave about 15mm uncut.

3 Write some jokes or riddles on a piece of paper. Include one in each bon-bon. Place a lolly or two and a trinket inside the tube. (Make sure these goodies don't fall in the middle slit.)

4 Cover tube with bright crepe paper. Leave 6-8cm hanging over each end, to be bunched up.

5 Decorate with stars, shapes, tinsel or Christmas stickers.

6 Tie the ends up tightly (as shown).

7 Test one with a friend.

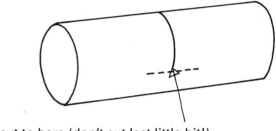

cut to here (don't cut last little bit!)

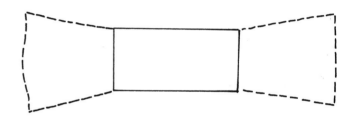

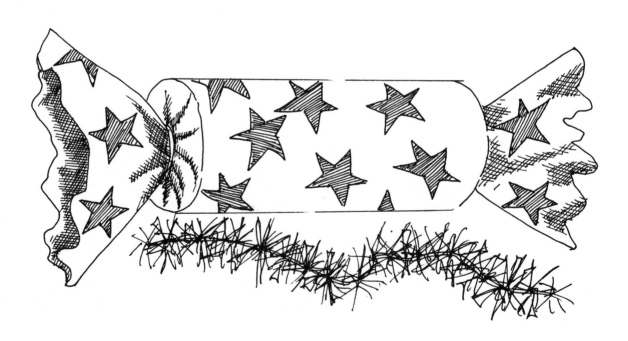